Disarming the Heart

Disarming the Heart

Toward a Vow of Nonviolence

John Dear
Foreword by John Stoner

Revised Edition

HERALD PRESS
Scottdale, Pennsylvania
Waterloo, Ontario

Library of Congress Cataloging-in-Publication Data
Dear, John, 1959-
    Disarming the heart : toward a vow of nonviolence / John Dear.—
Rev. ed. p. cm.
    Includes bibliographical references.
    ISBN 0-8361-3652-7 (alk. paper)
    1. Dear, John, 1959- . 2. Nonviolence—Religious aspects—
Christianity. I. Title.
BT736.6.D42 1993   93-28739
241'.697—dc20   CIP

The paper used in this publication is recycled and meets the minimum
requirements of American National Standard for Information
Sciences—Permanence of Paper for Printed Library Materials, ANSI
Z39.48-1984.

The Bible text is from the *New Revised Standard Version Bible*, copyright
1989, by the Division of Christian Education of the National Council of
the Churches of Christ in the USA, and is used by permission.

For my brothers,
David, Brian, and Stephen;

For my sisters,
Ita, Maura, Dorothy, and Jean

Contents

The choice today is no longer between violence and nonviolence. It is either nonviolence or nonexistence.
—*Martin Luther King, Jr.*

§ॐ॰

We are not allowed to kill innocent people. We are not allowed to be complicit in murder. We are not allowed to be silent while preparations for mass murder proceed in our name, with our money, secretly. . . . Thou shalt not kill; we are not allowed to kill. Everything today comes down to that—everything.
—*Daniel Berrigan*

§ॐ॰

I shall die, but that is all I shall do for death.
—*Edna St. Vincent Millay*

§ॐ॰

I have not the shadow of a doubt that any man or woman can achieve what I have, if he or she would make the same effort and cultivate the same hope and faith.
—*Mohandas Gandhi*

§ॐ॰

While you are proclaiming peace with your lips, be careful to have it even more fully in your heart.
—*Francis of Assisi*

§ॐ॰

Dear God, please enlarge our hearts to love each other, to love our neighbor, to love our enemy as well as our friend.
—*Dorothy Day*

A Vow of Nonviolence

RECOGNIZING the violence in my own heart, yet trusting in the goodness and mercy of God, I vow to practice the nonviolence of Jesus who taught us in the Sermon on the Mount—

> Blessed are the peacemakers, for they will be called [sons and daughters] of God. . . . You have heard that it was said, "You shall love your neighbor and hate your enemy." But I say to you, "Love your enemies and pray for those who persecute you, so that you may be [sons and daughters] of your Father in heaven." Matt. 5:9, 43-44

Before God the Creator and the sanctifying Spirit, I vow to carry out in my life the love and example of Jesus

- by striving for peace within myself and seeking to be a peacemaker in my daily life;

- by accepting suffering in the struggle for justice rather than inflicting it;

- by refusing to retaliate in the face of provocation and violence;

- by persevering in nonviolence of tongue and heart;

- by living conscientiously and simply so that I do not deprive others of the means to live;

- by actively resisting evil and working nonviolently to abolish war and the causes of war from my own heart and from the face of the earth.

God, I trust in your sustaining love and believe that just as you gave me the grace and desire to offer this, so you will also bestow abundant grace to fulfill it.

—*Pax Christi USA*

Foreword

We do not want to forget that we are God's children, but we do forget, each one of us. Nonviolence is a way of remembering and recalling, every day of our lives, who we are and what we are about—and returning to that truth of life whenever we forget.

—John Dear

REMEMBERING that we are God's children is the path by which John Dear invites us to nurture the spiritual roots of nonviolence. This book explores attitudes and actions characteristic of God's nonviolent children. It shows us how to disarm our hearts, so the world we imagine with our hearts can also be disarmed. "For out of the heart proceed the issues of life," said Jesus.

North Americans live in the most extravagantly armed society in history. We also live in one of the most extravagantly Christian societies in history. How has it happened that the professed followers of Jesus in the United States have led the world in producing the technologies of death?

Some may say that the only answer to the problem of war in the world and violence in the streets is conversion to Jesus Christ. Only when the hearts of people are changed is there hope of stopping war and violence, they maintain.

But in our situation people who have already been converted to Jesus Christ are leaders in the major institutional purveyors of violence. Christians play important roles in the U.S. military ("defense") establishment, the scientific research and development establishment, the military-industrial production establishment, and the multinational corporate arms trade complex.

In addition, people who have already been converted to Jesus vote for the politicians and pay the taxes which support this entire project of state-sanctioned violence. This does not inspire confidence that the change of heart effected by the typical Christian conversion is the full answer to the problem of war and violence.

Disarming the Heart describes conversion which does (and would) bring vital relief to humanity's massive suffering from injustice and war. It speaks of the conversion of the heart to the nonviolent way of Jesus. This is radical conversion—dramatic, thorough, and energizing.

In most lives such conversion takes some time. The church may have to abandon its preference for instantaneous conversions which leave the heart mostly unchanged. Needed instead are process conversions which disarm the violent heart and restore the image of God, who reaches out to enemies in forgiveness and love. Of course, however, the question is not really one of how much time but of how much change.

This is a book for people who care about people. It is a practical guide for the implementation of compassion. Herald Press is to be commended for publishing this revised edition of *Disarming the Heart*. Historic peace church writers have not produced a volume which gives sustained attention to the personal, psychological, and spiritual truths and disciplines by which individuals can hope to enter into and sustain a lifestyle of nonviolence. John Dear, a Catholic writer, has done this; the Christian community is indebted to him for it.

Want to make a difference for peace? Persuade your denomination to use this book to instruct its candidates for baptism, confirmation, or membership.

—John Stoner,
Akron, Pennsylvania;
coordinator, New Call to Peacemaking
and leader, GodQuest silent retreats

Acknowledgments

I WOULD like to express my gratitude to Peter Cicchino, Frank McAloon, and Parke Thomas, who shared with me the grace of vowing nonviolence on August 17, 1984.

I also want to express appreciation to Bill Sneck, Peter Cicchino, Monika Hellwig, Jack Marth, Eileen Egan, Mary Lou Kownacki, Harry Geib, Joe Sands, Charlie McCarthy, Donald Campion, Ed DeBerri, and Mary Evelyn Jegen who gave me suggestions and encouragement.

The life of Gospel nonviolence has been shown to me most clearly by my Jesuit brother Daniel Berrigan. Thank you, Dan, for your steadfast commitment to the way of nonviolence, for your friendship, and for helping me along the way.

I have also learned what commitment to Gospel non-violence means from the Jesuit martyrs of El Salvador, with whom I visited in 1985—Ignacio Ellacuria, Ignacio Martin-Baro, Amando Lopez, Segundo Montes, Joaquin Lopez y Lopez, and Juan Ramon Moreno. Thank you, brothers, for laying down your lives for the suffering peoples of El Salvador and the nonviolent struggle for justice. Your blood is the seed of Christ's peace.

For friendship, inspiration, and encouragement along the way of nonviolence, I also want to thank Jim and Shelley Douglass, Phil Berrigan and Elizabeth McAlister, George Anderson, Ken Butigan, Anne Brotherton, Pat and Ray Donovan, Patrick Hart, Richard McSorley, Martin Sheen, Valerie Sklarersky, Dean Brackley, Jon Sobrino, Jim Flaherty, Jim Gartland, Tom Hoffman, Tom Gumbleton, Lisa Goode, Billy Neal Moore, Ched Myers, Anne Montgomery, Richard Deats, Marie Dennis, Walter Sullivan, Bill O'Donnell, Jane Ferdon, Cindy Pile, Patrick Atkinson, Brian Willson, Gordan Zahn, and all my friends in Pax Christi USA, Bay Area Pax Christi, the Fellowship of Reconciliation, the Nevada Desert Experience, the Catholic Worker, the McKenna Center, Jesuit Refugee Service in Central America, Sojourners, and all my Jesuit brothers. I would also like to thank my parents, Margaret and David Dear.

Finally, thanks to John Stoner, David Garber, Michael King, and Herald Press for making possible this new edition.

This book is dedicated to my brothers David, Brian, and Stephen, and the North American churchwomen martyrs of El Salvador—Ita Ford, Maura Clarke, Dorothy Kazel, and Jean Donovan whose lives have been such an inspiration to me.

May the God of nonviolence disarm our hearts and make us instruments of God's disarmament of the world.

—*John Dear*
Washington, D.C.

Introduction

On a hot summer day, August 17, 1984, three friends and I climbed a hill in rural Pennsylvania, sat down in a shady place in the middle of four giant pine trees, offered prayers to the God of nonviolence, then each professed a solemn vow of nonviolence. We had prepared for this profession for nearly two years. We were excited as we began our celebration with songs to the God of peace.

We read Jesus' two great commandments to love God and neighbor, then we prayed, "Loving God, to you all hearts are open, all desires known, and from you no secrets are hid. Cleanse the thoughts of our hearts by the inspiration of your Holy Spirit, that we may perfectly love you, and worthily magnify your holy name. Help us to become instruments of your peace. We ask this in the name of Jesus our peacemaker. Amen."

We openly and honestly confessed our use of violence, our apathy in the face of systemic violence, our complicity in the structures of violence, and our failure to be people of nonviolence. A great stillness and calm came upon us. The Spirit of forgiveness and nonviolence was poured out on each of us in a very personal way as we took turns laying hands on each other and praying silently. We signed our forgiveness and reconciliation by embracing one another.

We recited psalms and scriptural readings, including a passage from Jesus' great sermon: "Love your enemies, do good to those who hate you, bless those who curse you, pray for those who abuse you. . . . But love your enemies; do good, and lend, expecting nothing in return. . . . Be merciful. . . . Do not judge . . . do not condemn. . . . Forgive" (Luke 6:27, 35-37).

We each reflected on our commitment to the way of nonviolence and how we had come to profess a vow of nonviolence. We spoke of the difficulties and risks it would involve, the great freedom it would open to us. We noted the solidarity with the poor, the humility, and the prayer needed to be faithful to God through the grace of the vow. We shared our thoughts about the need to be actively involved in resisting injustice and violence through loving nonviolence for the rest of our lives. We shared our commitment to support one another in the vow as well as our joy and consolation in knowing that nonviolence is an answer to the world's age-old questions about the meaning of life.

Our reflections reinforced one simple conclusion: Nonviolence is for us a way to God, to love, to truth. Our nonviolent God invites us to follow along that way of nonviolence all our lives. Let us then dedicate ourselves to becoming people of nonviolence, peacemakers, God's own children.

Before a simple wooden cross, each of us professed the following vow (which we wrote according to the tradition of our Community):

Loving God, Father of Jesus and Mother of all creation, you worked the salvation of the world through the life and death of Jesus and the outpouring of the Spirit. In his perfect act of suffering, nonviolent love, Jesus gave his life as a ransom for the many and redeemed his lost sisters and brothers from sin.

Trusting in your infinite goodness and mercy, before the cross of Jesus Christ, I vow perpetual nonviolence in fulfillment of the command of Jesus and in imitation of his holy life and death.

I seek the intercession of his mother Mary and all the saints and martyrs of nonviolent love.

Loving God, I trust in your sustaining love and believe that just as you gave me the grace to desire and offer this vow, so you will also bestow abundant grace to fulfill it.

As we made these promises, our hearts were filled with joy, consolation, the great love of God, and the hope that comes from the prospect of lifelong nonviolence. Our response was a joyous exultation of God, the Magnificat of Mary (Luke 1:46-55).

We prayed for peace in the world, for the poor and oppressed, for the end of injustice, and for the coming of God's nonviolent reign of justice and peace. We prayed in the words of Jesus for the coming of God's reign of nonviolence on earth as it is in heaven.

We closed with the plea,

God of perfect peace, violence and cruelty can have no part with you. May those who are at peace with one another hold fast to the goodwill that unites them; may those who are enemies forget their hatred and be healed.

Give us all the gift of your peace; make us into people of nonviolence. Make us instruments of your peace, channels of your nonviolent love.

Transform our hearts and transform our world, so that together, we may enter into your reign of nonviolence and see you face-to-face.

After a final blessing and praise, we broke into song.

For the four of us, this vow of nonviolence was a powerful, personal experience of the nonviolent love of God. We were embarking on a new course, opening a new door into the unknown realm of God's grace which would call us to be faithful to such a vow and to accept its consequences. We had not anticipated that the profession of our vow of nonviolence itself would prove to be such a beautiful gift from God. Our response was gratitude and praise. We realized we had been commissioned to be and to become instruments of God's nonviolence.

I felt my life was just beginning.

Nearly ten years have passed since that first profession of nonviolence. With Eileen Egan and Mary Lou Kownacki, I wrote a vow of nonviolence which Pax Christi (a national Roman Catholic peace movement) promoted and which thousands of people around the world have professed.

Personally my life has been turned upside down. I have tried to walk daily in the Spirit of nonviolence into the public world and its violence with the message of God's nonviolent alternative. As my family and friends will attest, I have failed again and again. I have given into the spirit of violence, apathy, and despair, and turned away from the grace that God offers.

Yet God continues to pick me up and invite me to start again along the road into God's reign of nonviolence. Every day I have recalled my vow and tried to begin again to live out the nonviolent love of God in my life and in the world. Every day I enter this Spirit of nonviolence who leads me deeper and deeper into God's own peace, into the very heart of God. God continues to disarm my heart and invites me daily to participate in God's disarmament of the world.

Through my vow of nonviolence, I have tried to say "Yes" to God's initiative, to God's disarming action of love. I want God to disarm me so completely that I become the human being God wants me to be, that I become who I already am—a beloved son of God, a peacemaker.

Through this vow, I hope God will transform my life, so I may spend my days in loving service to my sisters and brothers who suffer the violence of war, poverty, and injustice; in works of justice and peace; in active nonviolent resistance to systemic injustice and institutionalized violence. Thus I will participate in God's transformation of the world.

I want to help relieve humanity's suffering and uphold Jesus' vision of a new world of nonviolence. I want to be an instrument of God's peace. Ten years after professing a vow of nonviolence, I am just beginning to learn what that means.

I began to consider professing a vow of nonviolence while making the Spiritual Exercises, the thirty-day silent retreat of Ignatius Loyola. Deep reflection on the gospel of Jesus and how I could further accept God's disarming love brought me to realize that love is not compatible with violence in thought, word, or deed. Following Jesus meant a life of active nonviolence. Following Jesus meant a life of seeking justice, making peace, accompanying the poor, and resisting the systems of injustice and war through the way of nonviolence.

While making the Spiritual Exercises, I decided to study nonviolence and pray for the grace to know how God was calling me to be a follower of Jesus, a peacemaker. I spent over a year and a half considering the commitment and call of vowed nonviolence. I discussed the call with friends, experimented with it, and studied the lives and writings of the great practitioners of gospel nonviolence. This period of prayer, discussion, consideration, and study—mingled with service to the poor and the building of community—led me to want to accept God's disarming love wholeheartedly. I wanted to live that way of love and peacemaking with all my life.

Since that time, the vow of nonviolence has been a channel of grace in my life and work for peace and justice. With my friends, I have joined many experiments of nonviolent love across the country.

After I professed the vow of nonviolence at the Jesuit novitiate and retreat center in Wernersville, Pennsylvania, I moved to New York City. I served at a soup kitchen and shelter for the homeless, and studied philosophy at a Jesuit university. I joined *Kairos*, a community of active nonviolence in New York City. With my friends I attended vigils, leafletted, and risked arrest at the Riverside Research Institute (a center for the study and design of post-Cold War laser beam warfare).

In 1985, I traveled to El Salvador, where I lived and worked in a refugee camp in the middle of a war zone. The entire region was bombed every hour and U.S.-backed Salvadoran death squads roamed the area. I was questioned by death squads on more than one occasion. I had the profound experience of meeting thousands of Salvadoran *campesinos* (people of the land) who had suffered decades of oppression and warfare, yet maintained a steadfast faith in the God of peace and justice.

I also met with the Jesuit community at the University of Central America. Ignacio Ellacuria, the Jesuit president of the university, impressed me with his steadfast devotion to justice and peace, "to the coming of the reign of God in El Salvador," as he said. He urged me to continue to work for justice and peace.

I saw the bullet holes that lined their community house, heard stories of the many bombings they had survived and the countless death threats they endured, and learned again what a real commitment to the gospel of peace required. With heartfelt joy and trust in God, the Jesuits told me they were not afraid to die for the gospel. They would never give up their nonviolent struggle for peace and justice in El Salvador.

In the mid-1980s I taught history and theology from the perspective of Gospel nonviolence and from the perspective of the poor to high school students in Scranton, Pennsylvania. Then I moved back to Washington, D.C. (where I had grown up). There I joined the staff of the McKenna Center, a drop-in center and shelter for the homeless at St. Aloysius' church near the U.S. Capitol.

I met and befriended hundreds of homeless people. They suffered on the killing streets of Washington, D.C., while down the road, at the White House and the Pentagon, billions of dollars were spent on warfare and nuclear weapons. My friends and I took to the streets many times to ask that our society use its resources for the poor and the homeless. At the Pentagon, we called for renunciation of war and pursuit of a new society grounded in the principles of nonviolence, justice, and peace.

At the U.S. Capitol, we unloaded furniture in the middle of the street to demonstrate what an eviction looked like. We asked the Congress to dedicate itself to giving homes to the homeless and food to the hungry instead of continuing to fund the war-making industries of our nation. Over and over we were arrested and landed in crowded jail cells. But like the disciples in the Acts of the Apostles, we always returned to the scene of our crime with a new message of nonviolence, calling for conversion to the God of nonviolence.

In late 1989, I moved to Oakland, California, where I began four years of study at the Jesuit School of Theology, at the Graduate Theological Union in Berkeley. On November 16, 1989, my Jesuit brothers and Elba and Celina

Ramos were assassinated in El Salvador because of their outspoken, public commitment to Jesus' nonviolent reign of justice and peace. With Jesuits and friends from around the Bay Area, we gathered for prayer and reflection on the steps of the San Francisco Federal Building.

Some 150 of us, including eighteen Jesuits, knelt at the entrance in illegal prayer for the end of all U.S. military aid to El Salvador. We were arrested and spent the day sharing our life journeys and singing songs of peace and hope in a jail cell. In the weeks that followed, I was arrested for nonviolent civil disobedience at the Concord Naval Weapons Station, which sends U.S. bombs and bullets to El Salvador; at the Federal Building in Los Angeles with peacemaking friends; and at the U.S. Capitol as Congress debated U.S. military aid to El Salvador.

With Steve Kelly and John Auther (brother Jesuits), and two Salvadoran women, I embarked on a twenty-one-day fast for peace in El Salvador. Those days of prayer, fasting, and active nonviolence flowed from the ongoing experience of God's disarming action in my heart. They were the fruit of a life seeking to live Jesus' way of nonviolence. I trace all those days of grace back to that shining moment of grace which was my own vow of nonviolence.

In 1990 and 1991 I joined friends throughout the Bay Area and the nation in prayer, fasting, public speaking, and active nonviolence to resist the U.S. war in the Persian Gulf. In San Francisco, we marched for peace and risked civil disobedience at the Federal Building and at the Concord Naval Weapons Station, which shipped one-third of all the bombs dropped on Iraq.

On the first Friday of the war, we walked through the streets of San Francisco to mourn all those killed by the U.S. war machine. In the tradition of Martin Luther King, Jr., we knelt every few blocks along the way for silent prayer. When we arrived at the Presidio (the U.S. West

Coast Army Headquarters next to the Golden Gate Bridge), we were threatened with violence.

We knelt in prayer and invited our sisters and brothers in the U.S. military to lay down weapons and join us in opposing war. Some of us crawled over a stone wall onto the base and were arrested. Similar prayerful nonviolence continued in the Bay Area and throughout the nation.

Through the years, I have tried to offer solidarity with the poor, oppressed, homeless, and hungry; with those declared to be "enemies" of our nation. On several occasions, I have befriended people on death row and joined the public effort to oppose their executions.

With friends in the peace and justice movement, I am trying to break through the walls of racism and sexism so we can walk together into a new world of reconciliation. I have journeyed into the war zones of the Philippines, Guatemala, Nicaragua, the Middle East and Haiti. I have heard the testimony of the faithful who struggle for food, shelter, education, health care, justice, and a new world of nonviolent love. With my theology studies now completed, I have returned to my work for justice and peace among the poor and homeless in Washington, D.C.

Over the years, my friends and I watched as the Berlin Wall was taken down, the Cold War was declared over, and the arms race was supposedly ended. Yet we saw that people throughout the world were getting poorer, famines were raging anew, the United States continued to wage military intervention in the third world, and testing of nuclear weapons proceeded in the Nevada desert. The environment continued to hang on the brink of destruction. Funding for post-Cold War weaponry, continued to increase.

The world seemed to be changing every minute, yet it seemed to be the same. Things appeared to be getting better—but when I studied and analyzed what was really going on, things appeared to be getting worse.

As I write this, millions of people are starving in Africa while the U.S. continues to spend its resources on war and world domination. The violence that plagues our culture is reaching astronomical proportions, and our inner cities stand on the brink of explosion, as the 1992 riots in Los Angeles demonstrated.

During the 1980s and 1990s, the U.S. government spent hundreds of billions of dollars a year for war and nuclear weapons each fiscal year, yet funding for education, health care, the homeless, and AIDS research was cut. Over for.y wars are being fought around the world and over 60,000 children die from starvation everyday. Sexism, racism, greed, consumerism, torture, poverty and militarism tear our world apart. Even after the Cold War, our addiction to violence and death threatens to destroy us all. The need for a renewed commitment to the Way of nonviolence is more urgent than ever.

"I have not the shadow of a doubt that any man or woman can achieve what I have, if he or she would make the same effort and cultivate the same hope and faith," Gandhi, the apostle of nonviolence, once said. "We are constantly being astonished these days at the amazing discoveries in the field of violence," he continued.

> But I maintain that far more undreamt of and seemingly impossible discoveries will be made in the field of nonviolence. . . . My optimism rests on my belief in the infinite possibilities of the individual to develop nonviolence. The more you develop it in your own being, the more infectious it becomes until it overwhelms your surroundings and by and by might over sweep the world. . . . When the practice of nonviolence becomes universal, God will reign on earth as God does in heaven.

I believe Gandhi was right. Living out his vow of nonviolence, Gandhi declared, "I am prepared to die but there is no cause for which I am prepared to kill."

The words of Martin Luther King, Jr., hold true for us all: "The choice before us is not violence and nonviolence. It is nonviolence or nonexistence." We need to learn the ways of Jesus, to love our enemies, to seek justice for the poor, to speak the truth of peace, to put down our swords, to beat our nuclear weapons into plowshares of peace, and to become sons and daughters of God, brothers and sisters of each other. We need to commit ourselves anew to the way, the truth, and the life of nonviolence.

In God's realm there will be no nuclear bombs, Trident submarines, guns, and Pentagons; no torture, death squads, and wars; no famines, poverty, and homelessness; no apartheid, racism, and sexism.

My journey has been an effort to enter into the nonviolence of God. I long to continue the witness of nonviolence lived out publicly by Gandhi, King, Day, Merton, Romero, the Berrigans, and thousands of others around the world. I long to live the life of nonviolence modeled for us in the life of Jesus who continues to lead us.

I am not an expert on nonviolence; like everyone, I am a sinner. I am an expert at violence who struggles daily to walk the journey of nonviolence. Like everyone in this culture of violence, I am addicted to violence and struggle with a community of friends to become sober, to become nonviolent, to become peace-loving.

The journey of nonviolence, I am discovering, is an inner journey into the spiritual depths of nonviolence, into God. If I am open enough to the God who disarms my heart every day, my life, like the lives of all peacemakers, can become a nonviolent, spiritual explosion. My life can participate in God's transformation of the world into a realm of justice and peace.

My journey is one of transformation from violence to

nonviolence, hatred to love, war to peace, injustice to justice, death to life, into a world of peace where everyone
tries to be nonviolent. It is an inner journey that leads to an
outer journey and ultimately to the transforming God of
peace and nonviolence.

These simple reflections were written from my own
experiences. They view the vow as a way to enter the lifelong journey of nonviolence, a way to be faithful to Christ,
a way to cooperate with the God who seeks to disarm our
hearts and so disarm our world.

I wish to share this way of life with everyone, especially people of faith living in North America. Others may be
moved to profess a similar vow. I simply want to share a
way to God which I have found helpful. I write to those
drawn to nonviolence who have not considered a vow as
well as to those unfamiliar with the way of nonviolence in
general.

These reflections have proved a starting point for me.
In this book, after briefly reviewing what is meant by the
terms *violence* and *nonviolence*, I will examine vows and the
vow of nonviolence. Next I will look at reasons for professing a vow of nonviolence in our day and at implications of
the life of vowed nonviolence. Then I will explore further
questions about the very idea of a vow of nonviolence.

The book will conclude with reflections on Mohandas
Gandhi and Jesus. Gandhi was the great apostle of nonviolence who first professed a vow of nonviolence. Jesus is
and always will be the great preacher and model of nonviolence. It is to Jesus, the image of our nonviolent God,
whom we will finally turn to as we embark on our new life
of nonviolence. In the end, the vow of nonviolence is simply one way of following Jesus in today's world.

May these reflections be helpful for the journey into
nonviolence. May they encourage us all to accept God's
disarming love at work in our hearts and in our world.

Disarming the Heart

1

Violence Means
Forgetting Who We Are

ONE day in the mid-1980s, when I was working in a church-run refugee camp in war-torn El Salvador, I journeyed north to the province of Chalatenango to visit and pray at the graves of Ita Ford and Maura Clarke. They were the Maryknoll sisters murdered on December 2, 1980, along with Dorothy Kazel and Jean Donovan for their solidarity with the suffering Salvadoran people.

The bus I was traveling on, a typical old blue school bus crowded with campesinos, was stopped by the brutal U.S.-backed Salvadoran military. Everyone was ordered off the bus. Scores of Salvadoran soldiers wearing U.S. Army uniforms began searching us. The women were forced to line up in front of the bus, down the middle of the road, while the men lined up behind the bus.

It was a Sunday afternoon; there was no other sign of life. We stood in the middle of that narrow road, in a barren desert-like region surrounded by huge mountains far away on the horizon. Everyone knew that, in situations like this, the military death squads might at any moment round people up and "disappear" them—or shoot them on the spot. There we stood, somewhere in the north of El Salvador, surrounded by young Salvadoran soldiers holding machine guns aimed at us.

It was a normal road check. The soldiers were looking for guerrillas or weapons being transported to the revolutionaries. The soldiers' weapons were meant to intimidate us and protect them. They filled the air with fear. I realized any kind of accident could happen; I looked to see how the other Salvadorans alongside me were responding. They simply bowed their heads and stood in silence. They were praying they would not be taken or killed.

We were all searched one by one and asked our reasons for traveling in that part of the country. After a long time, we were permitted to get back on the bus and leave. I did not visit the graves of the martyrs because church people in Chalatenango warned me that soldiers would surely arrest me there and take me in for questioning.

On that day in El Salvador, I saw brothers and sisters acting toward one another as if they were objects or things to be feared or pushed around. I saw children of God—the Salvadoran soldiers—sadly trapped into a way of life that dehumanized others and themselves. I saw the effects of systemic injustice on a worldwide scale. I saw how imperial, institutionalized violence leads poor people to wage war against other poor people. I wept because of our violence toward one another.

This scene is typical of our world. In El Salvador, the guns and daily bombing raids killed scores of people and left an entire nation paralyzed with fear and poverty. El Salvador's repressive government was sponsored by millions of dollars from the United States.

Similar violence is aimed at the people of Guatemala, Nicaragua, Panama, Peru, and the Philippines. Elsewhere

—as in Haiti, Somalia, and India—entire populations hang on the brink of starvation, disease, and misery because they lack money, food, jobs, health care, and education. Their resources are controlled by the developed world.

On the streets of cities such as Washington, D.C., and of Los Angeles, people are gunned down every night in drug wars which are the natural consequence of a world given over to violence, injustice, and death. I have seen this suffering around the world. I have seen the headquarters for this structured violence in places like Wall Street, the Strategic Air Command Base near Omaha, the Pentagon, the White House, the Bangor Trident Submarine Base, and the Lawrence Livermore Laboratories. From the bombs falling on poor Salvadoran campesinos to the homeless on the streets of New York City to the people of San Quentin's death row, violence is always the same. It kills.

What Is Violence?

One way to define violence is to see it as the act of forgetting or ignoring who we are—brothers and sisters of one another, each one of us a child of God. Violence occurs in those moments when we forget and deny our basic identity as God's children, when we treat one another as if we were worthless instead of priceless, when we cling to our own selfish desires, possessions, and security.

The range of violence includes the self-hatred that flares in our hearts, the intentional harm we do to one another, and the systemic injustice that keeps hundreds of millions of people around the world in misery. Our apathy and indifference in the face of relievable suffering and our willingness to defend our possessions and self-interests without concern for suffering neighbors are forms of violence. Other varieties of violence are the lack of love in our hearts; the unwillingness to suffer with others in the struggle for justice; the pride that prevents us from forgiving others; and the insecurity, fears, and untruth in which we frame our lives.

Violence begins in our hearts as we give in to fear, despair, hatred, and anxiety; as we lose our inner peace, hate ourselves, and hate God. Whenever we forget or ignore the reality that we are all equal—all children of God, all brothers and sisters of one another, all loved unconditionally by God—then our hearts turn from love and peace to the chaos of hate and fear.

This negative state of forgetfulness feeds on itself, and soon we find ourselves without peace in our hearts. We arm our hearts against the God of love and against others. We fester in self-hatred and a lack of peace. Soon we start to lie, cheat, hate whole groups of people, and act selfishly. Communication with others breaks down. We forget the hidden ground of nonviolent love that we walk on; we act as if we do not recognize who other people are.

We no longer see the face of God in the faces of other people. Any common ground of equality or understanding vanishes. We are unable to see the world from the perspective of others and cling to our own absolute ideas of right and wrong. We lose concern for others, especially the poor, the marginalized, the oppressed, the suffering. We no longer hold the vision of a peaceful human family loved by a nonviolent God. We are blind and give in to the darkness of violence.

With these insights, Thomas Merton wrote in the early 1960s that "the root of all war is fear."

> At the root of all war is fear: not so much the fear people have of one another as the fear they have of *everything*. It is not merely that they do not trust one another; they do not even trust themselves. If they are not sure when someone else may turn around and kill them, they are still less sure when they may turn around and kill themselves. They can-

not trust anything, because they have ceased to believe in God.[1]

When we characterize others as enemies, when we look with fear and suspicion at others, we reveal the violence in our own hearts. We have forgotten who we are and to whom we are relating. When we respond to threats or acts of violence by retaliating with violence or by passively receiving the violence without insisting on the truth of our unity, we act against the unity already given to us by God. We are so blind that we know not what we do. We go against what is good for us by destroying the gift of peace already given to us. In our hatred, fear, and hostility, we wage war against God and the human family.

The violence in our hearts and in our world stems from this lack of love for ourselves, our sisters and brothers, and our God. It is grounded in self-hatred, fear, and lies. It kills our souls when it appears to protect and save our lives. With every refusal of God's gift of life and love, violence leads us not to security, as we may assume, but to spiritual death.

"Who dies first, the gunman or the victim?" Daniel Berrigan asks. The gunman, he answers.[2] "The nuclear weapons of communists may destroy our bodies," Richard McSorley wrote during the 1970s, "but our intent to use nuclear weapons destroys our souls."[3] Our preparation, threat, and willingness to kill others reveal how we have armed our hearts against our nonviolent God and given our very souls over to the ways of death.

To descend into violence is to spiral into nothingness and meaninglessness. It is to deny our existence and our meaningful identities as beloved children of God, where each one of us is equal and precious in God's sight. In violence we forget our God and act as if we have no God. When we reject love, truth, hope, and God in our everyday choices; in our complicity, apathy, boredom, and passivity; and in the bigger decisions of our values, employment, and lifestyles, we reject ourselves and the life we can lead together as children of God. Throughout history, violence has continued to lead to nothing but unhappiness, meaninglessness, despair, hunger, war, suicide, the design and use of nuclear weapons, the perpetuation of unjust social systems, and further violence.

When we descend this spiral of violence (as Dom Helder Camara calls it), we name each other not as sisters and brothers but as enemies, as inhuman objects. We label others "the enemy," objects of our hostility. As we start to perceive others as enemies, we arm ourselves further, give in to the spirit of violence, and encourage others to see us also as enemies, as objects.

Theologian Charles McCarthy defines an enemy as "one or many who negatively affect the survival of some self-interest," such as one's possessions, reputation, or power.[4] An enemy may threaten or actually harm ourselves, our friends, or our possessions. Quarrels and conflicts escalate as opposing people refuse to see each other as sisters or brothers, as images of God to be loved unconditionally and nonviolently. As positions are taken, each side insists it is absolutely right. With this conviction and unwillingness to listen, people feel justified in harming and ultimately killing one another.

Addicted to Violence

Once we forget who we are and begin to act violently, we legitimize the hurt we do and systematize our wickedness. We keep working at this legitimization to defend our perceptions, our use of violence. With the systemic violence of society, we encourage one another to be violent with one another, to relate to each other violently.

Like an alcoholic, we become addicted to violence. In

societies and cultures of violence, where everyone is addicted to violence, the ultimate infliction of death on
others—whether by gang murder, the mass murder of
warfare or the legalized murder of capital punishment—
becomes the standard way of proceeding. The abnormality
of violence becomes normal. Our cultural and worldwide
violence becomes a habit too ingrained to break. We are
unable to become sober. In our addiction to violence and
death, we are out of control.

Soon we wage world wars and threaten to destroy the
planet and all of humanity. Like those alcoholics who
eventually destroy themselves, this worldwide addiction
to violence reaches a point where the entire world is
threatened with destruction. When the U.S. dropped the
atomic bomb on Hiroshima and incinerated 130,000 people on August 6, 1945, we as a people crossed the line of
self-destructive global violence.

Though the Cold War is over, we still have tens of
thousands of nuclear weapons that can blow up the planet
several times. We still maintain a fleet of Trident submarines; each one can destroy whole continents of people.
We still participate in the forty wars being fought on the
planet. And we continue to prepare at the Pentagon and at
Livermore Laboratories for a postnuclear arms race—
where laser beam weapons (used in movies like *Star Wars*
or *Star Trek*) are being designed.

The nuclear arms race and its research center, the
Livermore Laboratories in California, are preparing for
"one thousand years" of research and preparation for nuclear annihilation. This was reported by Edward Teller, the
inventor of the hydrogen bomb, in a speech at Livermore
Laboratories on September 1, 1992.[5]

We are so out of control we think we can go on for one
thousands years with bigger and "better" weapons of mass
destruction. Meanwhile our culture and the world denies

its addiction to violence, claims the arms race is over, and that disarmament is around the corner. The world insists it is sober but is still drunk on violence. Like the alcoholic, we are so addicted that we have lost all basis in reality. We think we can go on forever with our global violence. In our massive, global denial, we do not think we will die. In reality, the planet and the human race continue to stand at the brink of destruction.

The Idols of Violence

Our original sin of violence has developed into armies that protect large groups and their possessions with mass violence and into the nation/state system that we have today that wields unparalleled violence. As we participate in national addictions to violence, we adopt patriotic and nationalistic symbols and ideologies which separate us from our sisters and brothers around the globe. We get caught in an uncontrollable, unreflected spirit which divides the human family.

We lose faith in God and no longer believe in the reality that we are all one human family. Or we invoke God's name in our wars against each other—as in the Persian Gulf War, where God was invoked by all sides to bless the bombings and killings. Once we find ourselves in such situations, we give into our despair and blindness. We fall further into despair, self-hatred, and violence against everyone. We lose sight of the vision of the global village, where all nations serve one another in peace and justice.

As we lose our faith in the God of peace and love, we create idols to take God's place. We no longer see the face of God in the faces of our sisters and brothers; we do not feel the nonviolent spirit of God among us. Our addiction to violence so blinds us that we think that our weapons of violence are our only hope, our only security. They become "gods of metal," as a Maryknoll film puts it. Our guns, tanks, "smart" bombs, "peacekeeping missiles," and nuclear weapons become our gods, our idols. We trust these idols and they justify our forgetfulness.

The nuclear arms race is a prime example of our idolatry; it is a primary sign of our addiction to violence. Forgetting that we are one family, we have greedily pursued our selfish interests, producing weapons of mass murder to protect our possessions. The result of this denial of God has been violence committed against the poor who suffer from hunger, disease, illiteracy, hopelessness, unemployment, and relievable misery. Our idolatry kills the spirit of peace and love within each of us, causes us to arm our hearts, to hate our suffering sisters and brothers, and to create systems of mass violence against the poor of the world.

Charles McCarthy defines violence specifically as "responding to a person as an object for the purpose of self-gratification. Violence is forgetting or ignoring that there is an infinity behind every human face."[6] When we deny the presence of God in another human being by not loving and serving all humanity, we are on the road of violence. We are forgetting or ignoring who we are, who we are called to be, and what we are about.

All of us forget who we are at times and so we all commit violence. All of us have been raised in the human addiction to violence. The struggle of life is not to accept and legitimize our forgetfulness, our violence. Our task is to repent of violence, to resist it, and to transform it by doing good, loving others, and becoming people of nonviolence. The challenge before us is to topple the idols of violence, and to worship living God of nonviolence.

The Institutionalization of Violence

The violence that happens when we forget or ignore our basic identities can take various forms on a continuum of violence, depending on the extent to which we have forgotten or ignored our basic identity. This spectrum includes any use of personal, emotional, psychological, communal, national, or international domination of one over another. Violence can range from the hatred that lingers in our hearts to the weapons that destroy humanity.

Our silence, apathy, and complicity in the systemic violence of militarism, the nuclear arms race, poverty, starvation, disease, hopelessness, the denial of human dignity, and other injustices are a participation in violence. The destitution and poverty which leads to the early and unjust deaths of the world's poor are caused by our greed, by multinational corporations, and by the arms race.

"Violence is a descending spiral ending in destruction for all," Martin Luther King, Jr., once said. He continued,

> The old law of an eye for an eye leaves everybody blind. Violence is immoral because it seeks to humiliate the opponent rather than win his or her understanding; it seeks to annihilate rather than to convert. Violence is immoral because it thrives on hatred rather than love. It destroys community and makes brotherhood and sisterhood impossible. It leaves society in monologue rather than dialogue. Violence ends by defeating itself. It creates bitterness in the survivors and brutality in the destroyers.[7]

Gandhi wrote long ago that poverty is the worst form of violence. Following this truth, Jesuit martyr Ignacio Ellacuria (assassinated in El Salvador on November 16, 1989), wrote of different stages of violence, beginning with the systemic violence that leads to worldwide poverty. For Ellacuria and the Jesuits of El Salvador, violence was first and foremost the structured economic systems that force the majority of people in oppressed countries into hunger, poverty, and misery.

Ellacuria maintained that the first violence that needs

to be changed is the "institutionalized, legalized violence of economic exploitation, political domination, and military might." [8] Ellacuria pointed out that the community of nations has been organized in a way that prevents the majority of people from getting basic necessities of life. This systemic violence is immoral, unjust, and sinful, he insisted.

From this structured violence follows a violence of repression. As people like the Jesuits of El Salvador begin to speak out against the structures of violence which benefit the few and kill the majority, they find themselves the targets of military regimes who protect the wealthy elite and big business. During the 1980s the violence of repression in El Salvador killed 75,000 people, while in neighboring Guatemala over 100,000 people were killed. Hundreds of thousands of people who have spoken for justice and peace have been tortured and killed throughout Latin America, Africa, and Asia. As Ellacuria observed, such repressive violence of military regimes almost always leads then to revolutionary violence. [9]

Reviewing these forms of violence, Thomas Gumbleton concludes that to be a peacemaker is to confront the unjust economic, structured violence which leaves millions of people in misery throughout the world. [10] The poor of the world ask us to transform the worldwide economic structures which kill them every day, so these systems can promote life and serve humanity. It is a challenge to remember that our sisters and brothers are dying because we have forgotten that they are indeed our sisters and brothers.

The Struggle to Remember

The struggle to be human today is a struggle to transform the forces of violence. It is a struggle to resist our addiction to violence, to become sober, to be people of nonviolence.

In the effort to claim our inheritance as loved children of God, we are invited to love one another. We are invited to resist death and choose life for all our sisters and brothers around the world.

In other words, we have to stop forgetting who we are. We need to *remember* who we are. We need to be aware of our identity as sons and daughters of a nonviolent, loving God who has already reconciled us. We have to choose the truth of reality. We have to say no to violence, to allow God to disarm our hearts, and to participate in God's disarming of the world.

We do not want to forget that we are God's children. But we do forget, each one of us. Nonviolence is a way of remembering who we are and what we are about, and returning to that truth of life. Nonviolence is noncooperation with violence, a refusing to forget. It offers a way toward the fuller life of love and community as God's beloved children. Nonviolence helps us be the beloved community of sisters and brothers God created us to be.

2

Nonviolence Is the Spirit of Love and Truth Which Remembers

ON January 30, 1956, a month and a half after the Montgomery, Alabama, bus boycott began, the home of Martin Luther King, Jr., was bombed. King was speaking at a church meeting when he heard the news. He sped home to find his wife, Coretta, and their two-month-old daughter, Yolanda, unharmed. The bomb had exploded on the porch and left broken glass all over the living room.

Montgomery had been filled with tension ever since December 1, 1955, when Rosa Parks refused to give up her seat to a white man and was arrested. After he was asked to help lead the boycott, King received many death threats. When the bomb went off, people were ready to fight back. A crowd gathered outside King's house. One man challenged a policeman, "You got your thirty-eight and I got mine. Let's shoot it out." Young men armed themselves with broken bottles and verbally abused the police. Montgomery was on the verge of a riot.

As the crowd continued to grow, King came out of his house and stood on the broken porch. His house was almost destroyed and his family could have been killed. He looked at the crowd and said,

> My wife and baby are all right. I want you to go home and put down your weapons. We cannot solve this problem through retaliatory violence. . . . We must love our white brothers and sisters, no matter what they do to us. We must make them know that we love them. Jesus still cries out across the centuries, "Love your enemies." This is what we must live by. We must meet hate with love.[1]

Slowly people started to leave. Later a police officer told a reporter, "I'll be honest with you. I was terrified. I owe my life to that preacher and so do all the other white people who were there." [2]

Martin Luther King, Jr., consistently chose to remember that his persecutors were his brothers and sisters; he acted within that reality of truth. Instead of giving in to the temptation to respond with further violence, he responded with love and respect—while still insisting on the truth of justice and peace.

Nonviolence is an attitude and a spirit of genuine love and truth toward all people in every situation which helps us to remember who we are and who we are called to be. Nonviolence is the peace of heart in which we love ourselves, our neighbors, all humanity, and God. It is the act of making peace, resisting death, and choosing life. It means living out of a disarmed heart.

Nonviolence refuses to cooperate with evil and resists injustice. It responds to each act of violence with goodwill and love while maintaining a commitment to the truth of justice. It is the willingness to suffer in the struggle for justice and peace without inflicting suffering on others or giving up the truth of justice and peace.

Five points comprise the spirit and way of life which is nonviolence.

1. Nonviolence Means Remembering We Are All God's Children

The first step is to remember we are all God's children, all equal brothers and sisters, all sons and daughters of God. From this worldview and understanding, all our acts of peace and justice follow. This remembering is the daily act of recalling our basic identities and living out of them. It constantly returns to God, allows God to disarm our hearts, and accepts the peace of heart that God offers.

As we accept God's disarming love every day we become more and more who we already are—beloved sons and daughters of God. In this disarming practice of remembrance, we live our lives in the Spirit of God, growing more and more aware at each moment of God's active presence in us, in the human family, in the whole world.

Once we remember who we are, we realize we could never hurt—much less kill—another person. We could never wage war, sit idly by while millions starve to death, or share in the systemic violence that leads to poverty and the arms race. This constant remembrance of the unity of all life calls us to renounce violence, no matter how noble the cause.

We come to see that violence is never justified, that there is no such thing as a just war. We understand that the means are the ends, that the way to peace is peace itself. In this attitude of life, we conclude with Gandhi, "I am prepared to die but there is no cause for which I am prepared to kill." Such is the basic decision of nonviolence: to choose life and promote justice no matter what—but without resorting to violence itself.

Because it is a constant remembering of the unity among all humans, nonviolence by its very nature involves community. It cannot be lived and practiced alone; it is not a rugged individualism but a participation in what Dr. King called "the beloved community of humanity." Nonviolence means participating in the re-formation of the local and global human community.

Nonviolence is not practiced in isolation, but in the messy world of violence. Active nonviolence remembers the human community in those places where our underlying unity has been forgotten, ignored, and divided. Active nonviolence confronts that forgetfulness with the good news of our reconciliation in God.

Nonviolence is every act of positive goodwill, rooted in the underlying unity of all people, that seeks justice and peace for all people. As Elizabeth McAlister writes, "Nonviolence is persistent reconciliation."[3]

2. Nonviolence Flows From Unconditional, Active Love

A second characteristic of nonviolence is that it is a spirit and force of love which is unconditional, non-retaliatory and sacrificial; a love which stands up and says "No" to violence and "Yes" to life.

Centuries ago, the Greeks used three words for love. *Eros* connoted romantic love and reciprocation. *Philia* expressed intimate affection between friends or the love returned because one is loved. And *agape* meant unconditional redeeming goodwill toward all women and men that sought nothing in return.

Agape love has no self-interest; individuals seek not their own good but the good of the neighbor. Nonviolence includes the fullness of agape—positive, active love for human good in ways that help, not harm.

Theologian Charles McCarthy observes that agape has

two main features. First is a willingness to suffer and take on the violence of others as we struggle for justice and peace and seek to transform evil into good—all without the desire for retaliation. Second is a willingness to serve others (especially suffering humanity) without the desire for reciprocation.[4]

Once we remember that we are all beloved children of God, then we put into practice this love of God. We try to right wrongs by loving others as our own brothers and sisters without hurting them, contributing to violence or seeking selfish ends (including service in return).

Agape is a selfless love that serves others and promotes justice. Unconditional, non-retaliatory love seeks to end violence and injustice everywhere. It says, like Jesus on the cross, "The violence stops here, with my own body and soul where it is transformed by love into love."

Nonviolence is the willingness, the choice, and the act of taking on the violence of others, suffering without retaliating, and freeing others from the trap of violence so they can love and be loved in return. Nonviolence breaks the spiral of violence by promoting the love of God. Nonviolence never strikes back, but stands straight, full of love and respect for others, insisting on God's truth. Nonviolence begins the transformation of the world into God's nonviolent reign of justice and peace. As Dr. King observed, unearned suffering is redemptive.

Agape is an attitude and a lifestyle of humble service to those who cannot reciprocate. Agape loves all people, particularly those labeled our "enemies." Agape loves those of us trapped in the spiral of violence.

Martin Luther King, Jr. stressed that "nonviolence does not seek to defeat or humiliate the 'opponent,' but to win friendship and understanding." Nonviolence, he said, "is directed against forces of evil rather than against persons who happen to be doing the evil."[5] Agape was central to

King's nonviolence. He defined agape as disinterested love especially toward the "enemy-neighbor" from whom no good could be expected in return, only hostility and persecution. King wrote,

> Agape is not a weak, passive love. It is love in action. Agape is not loving to preserve and create community. It is insistence on community even when one seeks to break it. Agape is a willingness to sacrifice in the interest of mutuality. Agape is a willingness to go to any length to restore community. It is a willingness to forgive, not seven times, but seventy times seven to restore community. If I respond to hate I do nothing but intensify the cleavage in broken community. I can only close the gap in broken community by meeting hate with love. If I meet hate with hate, I become depersonalized, because creation is so designed that my personality can only be fulfilled in the context of community. . . . Agape means a recognition of the fact that all life is interrelated. All humanity is involved in a single process, and all men and women are brothers and sisters. To the degree that I harm my brother, no matter what he is doing to me, to that extent I am harming myself. . . . If you harm me, you harm yourself. . . . When I am commanded to love, I am commanded to restore community, to resist injustice and to meet the needs of my brothers and sisters.[6]

King knew that nonviolence "avoids not only external physical violence, but also internal violence of spirit." King's nonviolence was grounded in a peaceful, disarmed heart. It was an attitude and a spirit free from violence. Such love loves everyone and does so publicly, breaking all categories and boundaries. It transforms everyone and reveals the love of God. Indeed, the practice of agape in the struggle of truth and justice proclaims the nonviolent coming of God on earth. Because it is based in unconditional love, nonviolence seeks to defeat injustice, not people.

3. Nonviolence Invites Solidarity with the Poor and the Oppressed

The active love of nonviolence invites us to love our enemies, to love all who threaten and therefore suffer at the hands of governments. We reach out with all our hearts to those under the gun of the oppressors.

The enemies of governments are the poor, the homeless, the hungry, women, children, the unborn, those on death row, and those with whom they wage war. Nonviolent love sides with opponents of our government, listens to their grievances, and works for an end to the killing so that our underlying unity may be revealed.

Nonviolence recognizes the face of God in the face of our government's enemies and sees these enemies as our sisters and brothers. Nonviolence understands that these seeming enemies can teach us how to be human, how to love, if we first love them with all our hearts. Nonviolence finds God in the enemy.

To live nonviolence is to find God everywhere in everyone. Since most of humanity suffers in misery and poverty and since God sides with the poor in their sufferings, as Scripture testifies, nonviolence calls us to side with the poor and the oppressed of the world. To promote justice for the poor requires that we walk with the poor, accompany the poor, and live in active solidarity with the poor.

Through solidarity we can learn to contribute to God's transformation of the systemic violence which kills millions each year. We can choose what the Latin American church calls "a preferential option for the poor."

Nonviolence sides with the poor and the oppressed and sees the world from their perspective; it pledges to follow their nonviolent lead in the transformation of the world. To accompany the poor is to enter into their life as best we can by living simply, giving away our possessions, and making their cause of justice our own. As Jesus showed this solidarity will mean entering into the power-lessness of the poor.

This preferential option for the poor, for the op-pressed, and for our enemies is an option for justice, rec-onciliation, and peace. It is a preferential option for the God who lives in and loves the poor, the oppressed, and the enemies of the world. Being sons and daughters of God means becoming like this God, our Mother and Fa-ther.

4. Nonviolence Involves Resistance and Truth

Nonviolence includes active resistance to violence and in-justice through a courageous, steadfast commitment to justice and peace. As the union of love and truth, nonvio-lence is a spirit and a way of active resistance to all that works against love and truth.

Nonviolence is not passivism or apathy; it is action that disarms, reconciles, and helps others to see that all are equal and meant to be treated with love and respect. Non-violence actively seeks to change evil into good through love and truth. To be nonviolent is to spend one's life lov-ing others and speaking the truth of justice and peace at all times.

Nonviolence as active resistance addresses violence and injustice everywhere—on personal, family, commu-nal, national, and international levels. This loving resis-tance insists that justice be done, that all killing cease, and that peace be given a chance. It promotes conversion, rec-onciliation and the beloved community at every stage. On the personal and family levels, nonviolence acts in a spirit of love and truth which consciously confronts violence and selfishness in others by drawing it out of them, deal-ing with it, and inspiring others to open their hearts and change their lifestyles.

The personal and communal witness of nonviolence,

while beginning with a spirit of love and truth in individual hearts, is always other-centered and public. Nonviolence is a process of disarming each other's hearts so we can be free from the bondage of violence and be instruments of the disarmament of the world.

On the communal, national, and international scale, committed nonviolence reveals the power of love and truth. If participants in campaigns of nonviolence have renounced violence in their own hearts, theirs can become a movement for the transformation of the world. Nonviolent movements dedicated to transforming systemic violence and injustice always work in the long haul, though they may appear to fail in the short term.

Nonviolent movements can take the form of vigils, fasts, protest marches, strikes, boycotts, tax resistance, and sit-ins. Nonviolent campaigns such as the resistance in Denmark during World War II, Gandhi's struggle for independence in India, and the U.S. civil rights movement have demonstrated the great potential of large-scale, nonviolent love applied to systemic injustice.

The nonviolent campaigns which toppled the Marcos regime in the Philippines, confronted China's tyranny, brought down the Berlin wall and brought down the Soviet Union make clear that if applied, nonviolence moves mountains. "The only thing that's been a worse flop than the organization of nonviolence," Joan Baez once said, "has been the organization of violence."

Nonviolence as public, active resistance to injustice and violence seeks to bring about the genuine good of all concerned. As Martin Luther King, Jr., explained,

> The nonviolent resister must often express his[her] protest through noncooperation or boycotts, but he[she] realizes that these are not ends themselves; they are merely means to awaken a sense of moral shame in the opponent. The end

is redemption and reconciliation. The aftermath of nonviolence is the creation of the beloved community, while the aftermath of violence is tragic bitterness.[7]

Conversion occurs when the aggressors recognize the common humanity in the nonviolent resisters who courageously suffer while resisting violence and demanding change. That recognition opens their eyes, disarms their hearts, and begins to transform systemic violence into justice and peace.

At the heart of nonviolent resistance is a commitment to truth. King and Gandhi both understood that nonviolence begins in the stillness of each person's heart, as he or she seeks peace and tries to live in a spirit of love. Truth-seeking begins with honesty with oneself and others and does not permit lying or cooperating with untruth.

As opposed to the moments of violence when we deny the truth and the falsehood of violence, nonviolence seeks to accept and fully embrace the truth and is thus lifegiving. In nonviolent resistance, the force of love allows others to see what is true and enables them to step more fully into the world of truth. The truth-seeking of nonviolence requires humility and openness. It refrains from judging people but judges violence wrong and proclaims the vision of nonviolence. When this combination of love and truth is pursued by large groups of people in the public arena, the nonviolent transformation of the world begins again.

Nonviolence is a way of living in truth and talking truth to others. Truth is often lost because our pride gives way to lies, hatred, and the harm people do to one another. But truth can become the rock of our existence. To seek truth, we patiently listen to others and accept new insight into truth with a spirit of peace. We change our ways and we suffer when necessary to help ourselves and others to see the truth more clearly. This nonviolent resistance to evil publicly proclaims the truth of justice and peace. It is thus risky, particularly in a world that denies its addiction to violence.

The first casualty of war is truth, as we saw in the Persian Gulf War. But the adage can be broadened—the first casualty in any act of violence is truth, the truth of our unity in God, our reconciliation. Because it insists on the underlying truth of the reconciliation already granted to us by God, active nonviolence opens the way to God's reign of justice and peace. It helps us to see God's truth, that we are all one, all God's children, already living in a world of peace and justice if we but accept it.

5. Nonviolence Is Rooted in Prayer

Nonviolence is impossible without God. A way of life that resists evil, speaks the truth, risks suffering and death, and enters into the process of global transformation relies entirely on God. It begins with prayer and is rooted and centered on God. Practitioners of nonviolence love God and seek to live in God's Spirit. They listen to God and allow God to disarm their hearts so that God can transform the world.

Nonviolence is a prayerful, lifelong journey that takes us deeper into the violence of the world and the sufferings of humanity where we encounter the fullness of God who is transforming us all. Nonviolence includes daily meditation on the God of nonviolence. This God loves us, disarms our hearts, fills us with peace, gives us hope, and empowers us to live the nonviolent way. This way embraces the loneliness of life, enters into solitude, daily contemplates the vision of a nonviolent world, and there encounters God.

This life of prayer and solitude of heart enables us to develop our relationships, to find peace with one another, and to transform our world. By centering ourselves in God every day and dwelling in God's peace, we can walk into the violent world with a disarming love.

"While you are proclaiming peace with your lips, be careful to have it even more fully in your heart," Francis of Assisi wrote.[8] Peace of heart is cultivated through prayer. "My greatest weapon is mute prayer," Gandhi wrote.[9] "Prayer from the heart can achieve what nothing else can in the world." [10] Active nonviolence is rooted in prayer, meditation, and the contemplation of nonviolence. As we allow God into our hearts, we allow God into the world. Prayer is the key to this new world of nonviolence, justice, and peace.

6. Nonviolence Is a Way of Transformation

Every act of nonviolent love helps us to remember that we are all children of God. With a sincere heart and a faithful desire to do the will of God, we can place all our trust in God. God will lead us as we try to become nonviolent, because God is nonviolent and has promised us these things.

This simple nonviolence can infuse mind, soul, heart, and body and become a way of life. Anyone can begin to cultivate a nonviolent spirit. Nonviolence is not an ideology, a strategy, or a technique—but a peaceful spirit, a path to be followed, a way of life.

We can never become perfectly nonviolent in this life. But through discipline, prayer, sacrifice, and community, we can approach nonviolence. With every risk of love and truth we take, no matter how small, we free others and ourselves to travel closer to a more peaceful world.

When we remember who we are and act out of that reality, our little acts transform our entire way of living with one another. We begin to find harmony in ourselves, in our relationships with others, and in our world. We allow God to disarm our hearts, and we participate in God's disarmament of the world. We try to live as unarmed people, followers of the unarmed one, Jesus of Nazareth.

Martin Luther King, Jr., responded freely, spontaneously, and nonviolently on January 30, 1956, when his house was bombed, and on many other occasions afterward, because he made a radical choice for nonviolence. It was a choice he continually made throughout his life. He did not turn from that choice, though he failed often and struggled with it daily. King was committed for life to the way of nonviolence. Because of this commitment, he could say over and over to those who supported injustice, war, and violence,

> We shall match your capacity to inflict suffering by our capacity to endure suffering. We will meet your physical force with soul force. Do to us what you will and we will still love you. We cannot in all good conscience obey your unjust laws and abide by the unjust system, because noncooperation with evil is as much a moral obligation as is cooperation with good, and so throw us in jail and we will still love you. Bomb our homes and threaten our children, and, as difficult as it is, we will still love you. Send your hooded perpetrators of violence into our communities at the midnight hour and drag us out on some wayside road and leave us half-dead as you beat us, and we will still love you. . . . Be assured that we'll wear you down by our capacity to suffer, and one day we will win our freedom. We will not only win freedom for ourselves, we will so appeal to your heart and conscience that we will win you in the process, and our victory will be a double victory.[11]

Because we so often forget who we are, some of us feel moved to profess publicly our commitment to nonviolence in order to help focus our hearts along the way of nonviolence. Before looking at what is involved in such a fundamental choice—a vow of nonviolence—the meaning of vows needs to be explored.

3

A Vow Is a Channel of Grace

VOWS have long been part of the Judeo-Christian tradition, from baptismal vows to the vows of marriage and religious life to private devotional vows taken in line with a person's calling. A vow is a deliberate, religiously binding, solemn promise made to God concerning some good taken after serious preparation and in full freedom.[1] A vow is a pledge to be faithful to a way of life, even through trials, difficulties, and temptations. Because it is a lifelong dedication to living out goodness, a vow can act as a channel of God's grace.

Vows are a sign of commitment to a new way of life, the beginning of a new journey that will deepen throughout the remainder of life. They are channels of God's grace already working in the person. As channels of grace, they allow the loving action of God to flow in and through a person.

A vow as a channel of grace can be a great support, helping those taking the vow to enter the way of life they have chosen and allowing that new way to be ingrained in their spirit. When difficulties arise, the natural response will be—in the manner of the vow—free and spontaneous. A vow is guaranteed to arouse difficulties and provoke danger because it is a pledge to another way of life, a deeper way that runs against the grain of human society. A vow helps maintain gospel values in contrast to the ways of the world.

Vows in Scripture

Vows appear throughout the Hebrew Scriptures. The first vow mentioned in the Hebrew Scriptures is Jacob's. He promised to worship God and to tithe in return for God's protection (Gen. 28:20; 31:13). Similarly, Absalom vowed to worship God (2 Sam. 15:7-8). A vow was often accompanied by a sacrifice, such as the burnt offering of a ram (Lev. 22:17-25; Mal. 1:14). When the people of Israel needed the special help of God, their vows, which were temporary, included not only a sacrificial offering but acts of self-denial. Fasting frequently accompanied a vow. Most important, as the book of Deuteronomy urges, vows to God should be fulfilled (Deut. 23:22-24).

Vows are mentioned throughout the Psalms as well. Psalms of thanksgiving sing God's praise for the deliverance from affliction and promise the fulfillment of vows. "Praise is due to you, O God, in Zion; and to you shall vows be performed," declares Psalm 65:1. In Psalm 66 we read, "I will come into your house with burnt offerings; I will pay you my vows, those that my lips uttered and my mouth promised" (Ps. 66:13-14). Psalm 66 ends with praise for God, "Blessed be God, because [God] has not rejected my prayer or removed [God's] steadfast love from me."

"My vows to you I must perform, O God," says Psalm 56:13. The psalm Jesus recites on the cross, beginning with the heartbreaking plea, "My God, my God, why have you forsaken me?" ends with a promise to fulfill one's vows: "From you comes my praise in the great congregation; my vows I will pay before those who fear [God]" (Ps. 22:25). A similar promise is made in Psalms 61:8 and 116:14, 18.

In the Acts of the Apostles, Paul fulfills a vow by cutting his hair, but we are not given any other information about the purpose of that vow (Acts 18:18). Paul also assists four men who have professed a vow (Acts 21:23-26).

The Vow of Baptism

Christians have been making promises at baptism since the first century, before the New Testament was written. Baptism itself was a vow to follow Jesus and his way of life and to reject Satan and his way of death. Vows arose in the history of the Christian community as instruments to renew the ideals and the call of discipleship made in Christian baptism. The commitment of baptism had become lukewarm, especially after the Christianity became legal under Emperor Constantine in the early fourth century. Vows were professed to help Christians live the radical demands of the gospel.

Historically in Christian tradition, vows have been instruments of repentance, encouraged by the Christian community to help Christians return to the hard road, the high ideals, the narrow path of the gospel. Vows were intended to and succeeded in shaking some Christians out of their comfortable lifestyles and into the uncomfortable lifestyle of companionship with Jesus.

Over the centuries, such vows of poverty, chastity, and obedience in community sparked a fire of renewal among those who professed them and may have helped maintain the faithfulness of the community. But with the institutionalization of the faith, the practice of the vowed life eventually lost some of its gospel spark as Christian communities became richer, more stable, more powerful, more secure, and less dependent on God.

Many who professed vows to God to be faithful to the way of the gospel became stuck in the temptations and cultural trappings of the times. Many Christians who made perpetual vows to God were less poor, less chaste, and less obedient (for example) to the demands of the gospel than the unvowed. Still there were noble exceptions. Francis of Assisi, most notably, vowed evangelical poverty and lived it for all to see.

For Christians a vow can be a pledge of commitment to the promises of faith made at baptism. Baptism is a pledge to begin a more faithful life of imitation and discipleship to Jesus Christ, a pledge to witness to Jesus' way of life. Through their baptismal promises, all Christians are called to the vowed life, to Jesus' way of life. The basic vow for the Christian is a vow of allegiance to the reign of God as revealed in Jesus Christ. Vows of truth, nonviolence, poverty, chastity, and obedience in community are part and parcel of the Christian commitment or vow of allegiance made at baptism. A vow is an explicit reminder of who we are as followers of Jesus, who we are called to be, and how we rely on God to live as God invites us to live.

Vows celebrate the commitment already begun—as beloved children of God. They are public expressions of the unity that exists, of the conversion that has occurred, and of the commitment that is underway.

Specific vows do not or should not create a level of higher commitment to following Jesus. Every Christian is called to live the life of the vows. Those of us who publicly vow are witnessing to the reality which already exists in our hearts. We thus profess our faith and gratitude to God and invite others to join this way of life.

The Witness of the Vow

Vows witness to another way of life. A vow for the Christian is a reminder of God's infinite love for every human being. Acts of love and truth will flow naturally from this reminder.

Vows bear the fruit of what has already been given by God to each of us. We take vows to some Godlike way of life, such as nonviolence, to remind ourselves of God's gift of nonviolent love, to highlight that particular mandate of the gospel.

The vows can not be lived apart from the faith commitment in our heart which keeps us searching for God. Vows are an intricate part of the human life we are all called to live. A vow therefore invites all people to live according to God's ways, to become the people we are called to be.

In reality, Christians do not "make" a vow; we affirm the reality of a vow already made by God. Vows help us to witness to all that God is doing for us and for the whole human family. God has vowed to love and support us forever. Therefore, by pledging ourselves to poverty and nonviolence as God's way of life, for example, we are not "creating" the vowed situation. We are merely witnessing to the fact of its reality in our lives.

The vow should not be looked on as something we do for God, but as something God is doing in our lives. Christians have already experienced the disarming love of God. In a vow of nonviolence, we publicly proclaim this disarmament and commit ourselves to pursue it all our lives. To profess a vow is to witness publicly to God's love for us and to God's reign of justice and peace. We profess vows to God's way of life—in this case, God's nonviolence—to be a sign of that love, that way of life, in the world.

Vows formally dedicate ourselves to a way of life in imitation of God and are pledged to God—but also to all humanity, to our community, and to ourselves. Vows by their very nature should free us to become more fully human, alive, and at the service of others. Vows are thus other-directed yet serve to maintain a person's freedom in the way of life chosen—forever. They become instruments of freedom and release persons to be who God wants them to be. In this way, a vow can help us become "light of the world" and "salt of the earth," as the gospel suggests.

Vows Help Free Us

While a vow can help a person hold fast to a great commitment, a vow is not a new legalism. A vow does not begin a life of rigid adherence to a set of laws; rather, a vow breaks any rigid set of laws in our life. A vow stimulates us to risk development in one particular facet of life, to risk growth in God's spiritual way of life. Vows bind us to a higher law—God's law of love and truth which demands dependence on God. Because of its spiritual and practical nature, a vow will be dangerous and ultimately impossible to fulfill. It becomes the ideal by which we continually act in thought, word, and deed.

Vows free us to be God's loving sons and daughters. The vow itself can give energy and encouragement to persevere in freedom in the way of God.

Vows create the radical instability and insecurity of strict dependence on God. This is the freedom which vows can release—strict obedience to God's way of living. Vows recognize that to be fully human we can no longer rely on human structures or institutions but on God alone. Vows promise conscious, risky reliance on God. Vows as instruments of God's grace can release us from human structures so God will live more fully in us.

Vows are not coercive by nature. They do not subject us to some punishing authority, such as the church, a religious community, or to our own determination to enforce the vow and punish infractions. Fear and coercion have no place in the nature of a vow. A vow is freely professed and lived. Fear and coercion have no place in the discernment, profession, or practice of the vowed life.

When we suspect fear or coercion in the vowed life, we are to act against this in the freedom of grace and to live the life God desires. God does not act through fear or coercion. As channels of God's grace, vows cannot be lived in fear or coercion either. In this sense, vows can be channels of our liberation.

Vows Strengthen Us to Be Who We Are

Like baptismal promises, vows express the kind of person we want to be, the person God invites us to become, the life of God we wish to live. Unlike oaths (which usually invokes God as a witness to truth and thus implies God may punish the person), baptismal promises and evangelical vows are made to God and to one another as expressions of our deepest desires about who we want to be. They are prayers of petition, asking God's help to become what we believe God has called us to be. As channels of grace, they can strengthen us in this new way of life.

When offered in community, vows can become a bond of love, as marriage vows bind two people in love to love. The vows become part of the friendship that is community. A vow pledged in community may make the commitment more memorable, more deeply ingrained into our being as a new way of life to be lived. Communal celebration of a vow can be part of the vow itself, providing spiritual motivation, support, strength, and freedom so we can live even in the most challenging situation tempting us to break the vow.

A communal celebration of a vow can be a witness and source of strength to the community itself. The vow can be a channel of God's grace to every person who becomes a witness of what God is doing in the newly vowed person.

A vow professed in community and lived out with God, our community, and ultimately the entire human family, can become a great sign to the world. Such a vow calls the world to a new way of life, to greater freedom, and to a deeper awareness of God's reign. A vow has the possibility of being a great tool for the service, disarmament, and redemption of humanity and is thus worth serious consideration and discernment by all.

A vow publicly symbolizes the acceptance of and commitment to God's call to be who we are. A vow to God's way of life, made in freedom and without fear and coercion, is a gift from God. Faithfulness to such a vow is also a gift from God. It can be maintained only through diligent effort, constant attention, community, and regular prayer—but ultimately, through God's grace.

Any vow to a way of life is impossible to keep without God. Yet through the desire and will to cling to the pledge, we may be freed to live the path chosen and to enter into the life we have been called to live. This is the paradox of the vowed life. The vow can help us live a seemingly impossible way of life in today's world, yet it is not our action that fulfills the vow but the grace of God at work in us. The vow reminds us that it is God who is acting, living, and moving in us, that God reigns in our hearts and in the world—indeed, that God is God.

In a world addicted to violence, the promise of nonviolence may help us break through our denial and our addiction to become sober. In a world of war, starvation, systemic injustice, and nuclear weapons, some people may need to concretize their life commitment to God's way of active nonviolence by professing a vow of nonviolence.

Such a vow can be a channel of grace to help us become a people of nonviolence in a world of violence. Let us next review why some of us may be moved to profess a vow of nonviolence.

4

The Need for Great Love in a Time of Great Need

NONVIOLENCE maintains that violence is not morally acceptable on any grounds. It insists that violence is never justified. Every human being is a victim of violence and needs to be freed from violence. Nonviolence is the way to global healing. To be fully human is to become nonviolent. To live humanly is to renounce violence and embrace nonviolence.

There are many reasons for professing a vow of nonviolence. It may be helpful to probe the forces of violence at work in our day.

The violence of our world is real; it is what El Salvador's Jesuit theologian Jon Sobrino calls "real reality." The world's violence is not some abstraction that occurs far away and does not concern us. Violence committed anywhere toward anyone is violence done to us, to our brothers and sisters, and to God. Violence hurts both victims and victimizers and needs to be transformed by our love, by our willingness to take on suffering, by our insistence on the truth of peace. The systemic violence of our governments in which we participate is real. We are all called to accept responsibility for it and put an end to it.

After briefly looking at the realities of violence in our age, we shall consider some specific personal and communal graces a vow of nonviolence has to offer. A vow of nonviolence is a grace given to us by God as a means of reform and renewal on all levels—spiritual, personal, intellectual, theological, interpersonal, communal, national, and international. As we explore why some choose the vow, we may realize more fully who God is, how nonviolent God is, and how God revealed in Jesus invites us into nonviolence.

To break our addiction to violence, we need to look coldly at our violence. We need to admit that we are addicted to violence, break our denial of violence, and begin the process of transformation into nonviolence.

Recognizing Our Addiction to Violence

The personal, national, and international crises of today's world call for a new way of living. If there ever was a time for people to vow nonviolence for the transformation of the world, now is the time.

Over sixty thousand people, primarily children, die of starvation every day. Over forty wars are being waged as of this writing. Over 2 million dollars are spent on weapons of death every minute. Over one billion people are displaced and homeless. Three-fourths of humanity suffer in poverty and misery. Destruction of the ozone layer, rain forests, and oceans threatens the survival of the planet. Torture, sexism, and racism are national policies. Over twenty-five million people have been killed through legal abortion in the United States since January 22, 1973. And nations legally execute people by the hundreds.

In such a world, it is necessary for some people to commit themselves wholeheartedly to nonviolence. In such a world, a vow of nonviolence can be a channel for the transformation of many and even of the world. The vow of nonviolence can witness the alternative of nonviolence. For the Christian, the vow of nonviolence makes explicit what is implicit—that God loves every human being unconditionally and invites us to love each other in the same way.

Given our addiction to violence, the human family is trapped in a descending spiral of violence and is powerless to turn around without a concerted effort and communal, international commitment. Our world has become so unfairly structured that violence among people has become the norm.

The United States, for example, has become, in the words of Martin Luther King, Jr., the greatest purveyor of violence in the history of the world. With only 5 percent of the world's population, it controls over 60 percent of the world's resources. Twenty percent of the world's population controls 80 percent of the world's resources, while 80 percent of the world's population has nothing or next to nothing. Most human beings live in poverty and misery. The common experience for most people in the world is to wake up in the morning and wonder if they will survive the day. For most middle- and upper-class North Americans, survival is not a daily concern. This structured injustice is the breeding ground of violence. The greed and fear behind it are the roots of our worldwide addiction to violence.

"If we want to own things, we must also have weapons," Francis of Assisi observed. "From this come all the quarrels and battles that make love impossible. And this is why we refuse to own anything."

The systems and spirit of violence which divide us and turn us against one another cause us to forget that we are all one, all equal, all God's children. The wealthier classes are determined to maintain their wealth, to make more money, and to control the world's land and natural resources at the expense of others. The largest owners of the world's wealth and natural resources, the banking and investment systems throughout the world, seek to control and increase their wealth by influencing governments to protect their assets through the use of massive violence.

Because of the systemic greed of a minority of people, wars have been fought and weapons of mass destruction developed. In the United States, one/two-hundredth of the population owns and controls 37 percent of what the nation produces. This elite group of billionaires and millionaires defends its unjust command over society and the poor through an unprecedented military-industrial complex that threatens to destroy the planet, even after the Cold War.

The U.S. has legally spent over 11 trillion dollars on making war and killing people since 1946. The U.S. budget for fiscal year 1993 included over $232 billion for warmaking purposes. The world spends over 900 billion dollars each year on war and killing people. A fraction of those funds could end world hunger in two weeks, house the world's homeless, prevent diseases, and improve life for millions of people. If one-tenth of this money were diverted to world needs, it would be more than the total amount the World Bank estimates would wipe out world hunger.

The Reagan administration spent 1.14 trillion dollars for war between 1984 and 1987. One trillion dollars is a lot of money. How could that money have been spent differently? Here is one answer.

> For one trillion dollars, you could build a $75,000 house, place it on $5,000 worth of land, furnish it with $10,000 worth of furniture, put a $10,000 car in the garage and give all this to each and every family in Kansas, Missouri, Ne-

braska, Oklahoma, Colorado, and Iowa. Having done this, you would still have enough left to build a $10 million hospital and a $10 million library in each of 250 cities and towns throughout the six-state region. After having done all that, you would still have enough left from the original trillion to put aside, at 10 percent annual interest, a sum of money that would pay a salary of $25,000 per year for an army of 10,000 nurses, the same salary for an army of 10,000 teachers, and an annual cash allowance of $5,000 for each and every family throughout the six-state region—and not just for one year, but for [generations to come].[1]

The world's systemic violence results from blind obedience, a naive acceptance of and tacit indifference to systemic violence, and a complete misunderstanding of the unity of human life. Such global violence is the natural consequence of our unwillingness to forgive each other, to accept God's gift of peace, and to be healed from the violence we do to each other. The great sin of our apathy in the face of relievable human suffering and misery around the world reveals the depth of our violence.[2]

The U.S. system of imperial violence is the extreme consequence of the nation/state system and military force. Millions of human beings around the world are engaged in the preparation, study, planning, and strategizing of war, as well as in the actual fighting of war. Governments, cultures, and military forces have become abstracted from the actual killing of human beings.

Our addiction to violence is so great we give the greatest honor and glory to those who kill, and lead in the killing of, the most people. Military forces are exalted for "serving their country and the world" when they prepare for war and carry out the slaughter of other human beings. The ultimate purpose in any military force is always the killing of other human beings. We rarely admit the first priority of our military force is the capability to murder large numbers of people. Indeed, in the U.S. to join the army's campaign of murder is to "be all that you can be."

With the existence and continued development of nuclear weapons and the postnuclear weapons of laser-beam warfare, the possibility of killing millions of individual human beings in a nuclear war remains. The time, money, and human talent spent on building and maintaining these weapons actually oppress human beings into poverty, hunger and early deaths. Our addiction to violence has resulted in death, grieving families, despair, destruction, broken families, orphans, widows, widowers, wounded people who will suffer for the rest of their lives, and casualties on all levels of society.

A Century of Violence

In the twentieth century, organized and systemic violence reached global proportions that have threatened to destroy us all. In World Wars I and II, millions died in senseless horror. In World I, religions and church groups supported mass murder by their governments. In World War II, fifty million human beings were killed. In the U.S. and Europe, this war was declared "just" by church people on all sides.[3] In German concentration camps, millions of people were incinerated and killed. Firestorms from Allied air power killed 155,000 men, women, and children in Dresden in February 1943; 50,000 in Hamburg in August 1943; 12,000 in Darmstadt in September 1944; and 25,000 in Berlin in February 1945.

On March 9, 1945, 333 B-29s destroyed sixteen square miles of Tokyo with incendiary bombs and killed 130,000 men, women and children. The next night, 313 planes, using napalm, set fire to Nagoya, Japan's third largest city. On May 23 and 25, B-29s began another firestorm which killed thousands and destroyed seventeen additional square miles of Tokyo. As the fire bombings continued in

Japan, killing thousands more, *Time* magazine described the bombings as a "dream come true." [4]

On Monday, August 6, 1945, the atomic bomb was dropped on Hiroshima, killing over 130,000 men, women, and children instantly. The seventh largest city in Japan, Hiroshima had been spared the summer's fire bombings so U.S. military planners could see the effects of the atomic bomb on a relatively large and untouched city.[5]

The bomb dropped by the U.S. on Nagasaki three days later killed over thirty thousand more people. The U.S. justified these massacres by insisting they were necessary to end the war and "save the lives of U.S. soldiers." Decades later, we now know that the U.S. government dropped those bombs and killed those people not to end the war and not to force the Japanese to surrender (the Japanese were about to surrender and the U.S. knew the war would be over within a matter of days). The goal was to send a signal to the Soviet Union that the U.S. was now the number one military power in the world.[6] In reality, World War II never ended; it developed into the nuclear arms race.

Since 1945, the U.S. and the former Soviet Union have produced hydrogen bombs which have the destructive force of over fifty times the bomb used on Hiroshima.[7] Over 55,000 nuclear weapons have been constructed, enough to blow up the planet fifteen times over.[8] The U.S. and the Soviet Union never intended to stop the arms race; it allowed them to control the poor of the world and to maintain unfair control over the world's resources.

Since 1945, the world has come to the brink of nuclear war twenty-eight times. Great Britain, France, China, and India have each exploded nuclear weapons. Argentina, Canada, West Germany, Israel, Italy, Japan, Pakistan, South Africa, Sweden, and Switzerland can all build nuclear weapons. Other countries that want to develop nuclear weapons include Australia, Austria, Belgium, Brazil, Denmark, Egypt, Finland, Iraq, Libya, Netherlands, Norway, South Korea, Spain, and Taiwan.

Because of the proliferation of nuclear weapons, nuclear war could start almost anywhere. Today the U.S. can destroy every city of one hundred thousand or more people in the former Soviet Union at least thirty-six times. The weapons of the former Soviet Union can destroy every U.S. city at least eleven times.[9]

Since World II, the direct cost of the arms race has well exceeded 6,000 billion dollars ($6,000,000,000,000). The total megatonage now deployed is estimated to be equivalent of over one million Hiroshima bombs—or three tons of conventional explosives for every person on earth. About 25 percent of the world's scientific personnel are engaged in military-related pursuits.[10] The cumulative effect of nuclear weapons being exploded and stored around the country has been devastating to the environment, possibly causing permanent damage.

Our addiction to violence and death has brought us to the edge of global annihilation.

The Violence Continues

Today, despite the collapse of the Soviet Union, the end of the Cold War, massive human suffering around the world, and the threat to the Earth itself, the U.S. and other nations still develop, maintain, and create weapons of mass destruction. Though the U.S. and Russia agreed to reductions in strategic nuclear weapons (11,400 to 3,500 weapons for the U.S., 10,600 to 3,000 for Russia); though intermediate-range missiles and some ICBMs have been destroyed or partially deactivated; though SAC bombers have been taken off continual alert—the arms race still affects us. The U.S. still holds the nuclear gun to the world's head. Nuclear weapons and military installations are spread over every congressional district in the land.

We continue to maintain a military economy where our number one business is killing people and helping other people kill people. In the late 1980s, two former secretaries of state, Kissinger and Brezinski, issued a report to Congress calling the U.S. policy in the post-Cold War era, "discriminate deterrence." The goal was to prevent social revolution in and maintain control of less developed countries.[11]

Meanwhile we continue to build a fleet of twenty-one Trident submarines carrying 1,728 nuclear warheads—a program of death costing $100 billion. Each Trident submarine (at a cost of $2 billion) carries the equivalent of 6,400 Hiroshima bombs or twenty-five times the firepower used in World War II. The cornerstone of U.S. warmaking, Trident is intended solely as a first-strike weapon.[12] Why does this continue?

Our addiction is still not under control. Indeed, as with all addictions, our addiction to violence will not go away. It is a lifelong process to become sober. Not only have we not yet become a sober people of nonviolence, we have yet to admit our addiction.

The Bomb Has Already Gone Off in the Third World

The spending of massive global resources on developing these weapons of mass destruction is directly related to the suffering of most people around the world. The starvation of people in Africa, for example, is like a nuclear attack already waged against them. In eastern Africa, 23 million people face starvation in the 1990s. This is because during the Cold War the U.S. and the Soviet Union both wanted military bases in the region, the U.S. supported brutal dictatorships, wars uprooted millions of people, farming ceased, and people were displaced. In southern Africa in the 1990s, 30 million people risk starvation because of a drought that has ruined crops and emptied water holes.[13]

Instead of working creatively to solve this international suffering with the help of massive funding, the U.S. and other developed nations have continued to spend their energies and resources developing and maintaining systems of war and injustice. Millions of men, women, and children are deprived of basic living needs, including food, clothing, shelter, medicine, and education. They live in absolute poverty. The nuclear arms race and the works of violence to which we all contribute are directly connected to this global suffering.

The Conventional Violence of War

Conventional warfare, U.S. military intervention, and so-called low-intensity conflict continue to kill and do violence to peoples everywhere. The wars in Ireland, Afghanistan, Cambodia, Angola, Liberia, the Philippines, India, Vietnam, Korea, Iran, Iraq, the former Yugoslavia, Honduras, Peru, East Timor, and Haiti have brought misery, oppression, and death to countless millions of people. The Pentagon, the Central Intelligence Agency, and the U.S. military have been directly or indirectly involved in every one of these wars.

In Latin America alone, the U.S. has a long, bloody record of supporting brutal military regimes and juntas that have killed hundreds of thousands of poor *campesinos*. In Nicaragua, the U.S.-supported the brutal, unjust Somoza dynasty for decades. When a reform government took power and began to meet the needs of the poor, the U.S. immediately waged war against Nicaragua, not only to kill the Nicaraguan people and end the progressive government, but to set an example to all less developed nations that the U.S. will not tolerate systemic reforms.

The victims of these wars always tend to be poor, oppressed, marginalized peoples just trying to survive. The U.S.-sponsored government death squads of El Salvador murdered over 75,000 poor men, women, and children from 1979 to 1992.[14] On May 14, 1980, six hundred people, mostly women and children, were massacred in the waters of the Sumpul river by Salvadoran and Honduran troops—both armed by the United States.

When I lived in El Salvador during the summer of 1985, I worked in a refugee camp with poor Salvadorans who had lost their homes, family members, and friends. We watched and listened as U.S. and Salvadoran airplanes bombed and machine-gunned a nearby mountain and its inhabitants. On trips to the Middle East, the Philippines, Guatemala and Nicaragua, I have also seen the U.S. war machine at work.

The Iran-Iraq war of the 1970s and 1980s left over one million people dead. The U.S. supplied weapons to both sides and made a huge profit from the massacre of these peoples.

The 1991 Persian Gulf War left over 200 U.S. soldiers dead. Over 200,000 Iraqis are estimated to have been killed. Over 100,000 children died in subsequent months from disease and injuries due to the war. The "mid-intensity" weapons used by the U.S. in this war were the equivalent of one Hiroshima bomb a week dropped on Iraq.

The U.S. held hundreds of nuclear weapons on ships in the Persian Gulf during the war, and several U.S. government leaders hinted at the possibility of using those bombs on Iraq. At the end, in late February and early March 1991, tens of thousands of fleeing Iraqi soldiers were bombed along Highway Five as they fled Kuwait. In a massive reenactment of the My Lai massacre, the U.S. killed tens of thousands of people by burying them alive in ditches.

While the U.S. economy was declining and funds for

housing, education, and health care were being cut, the warmakers who sponsored this war profited enormously. California's Concord Naval Weapons Station, for example, had a 121 percent profit in 1991 thanks to the slaughter of the Iraqi people.[15]

The Myriad Forms of Violence

Abortion, capital punishment, and torture also continue to kill thousands of people. In the U.S., countless unborn children die every year by legal abortion. Every year in the U.S. and elsewhere, more and more men and women (primarily African-American men) are killed by gas, lethal injection, or electrocution. Following the inconsistent illogic of violence, the U.S. kills people who kill people to show that killing people is wrong.

Torture is practiced by many governments around the world. Millions suffer the violence of displacement, becoming refugees in their own homelands or in other countries. Sexism and sexist structures oppress women throughout the world. The domestic violence of men against women has killed and injured countless women.

Racism continues to kill and divide the human family. The effects of systemic racism in our own country were demonstrated with the Simi Valley verdict that the police officers who beat Rodney King were not guilty of any crime. The violent rebellion that followed in Los Angeles in April 1992 is a sign of the underlying violence erupting in our society.

In Western culture, violence pervades almost every aspect of life. Television programs and movies promote violence and portray violent people (Rambo, Batman, the Terminator) as heroic and admirable. Magazines advertise and spread violence. Many cartoons, toys, comic books, and other products for children promote and advocate violence. Meanwhile, the media plays up the violence of the world to sell newspapers and commercials. General Electric, the third largest nuclear weapons manufacturer in the world, owns and operates NBC television and thus determines what is news.

Most of us feel helpless and overwhelmed in the face of such institutionalized violence. Our addiction to violence convinces us nothing can be done to prevent violence, to end the arms race, to stop war. Indeed, according to society's definition, sanity has come to mean cultural approval and conformity, no matter how serious the complicity in violence, no matter how close we are to environmental and nuclear destruction.[16]

Once we are willing to blow up a city or the world, to push the button that will start a nuclear war, to destroy the planet, to maintain one Trident submarine, to shoot one person, or to allow one person to starve to death—we will do anything. Our addiction to violence is out of control. We are very ill, approaching spiritual death, as Dr. King observed. Our only hope lies in the way of nonviolence.

Confronting Violence with the Power of Nonviolence

The God of nonviolence calls us to face our violence, to admit our powerlessness to our addiction to violence, and to turn completely to God. Instead of striving for success, fame, wealth, pleasure, power, and global domination; instead of continuing to support the structures of violence and the wars of the world, we are summoned to speak publicly against violence. We are encouraged to live according to the purpose for which we were created—to know, love, and serve the God of peace, and thus to love one another. We are asked to form movements of nonviolence that will transform our world.

A movement for peace and justice is sweeping through the churches and religions of the world. Despite the overwhelming odds, people are beginning to stand up for justice and peace in the spirit and way of active nonviolence. In the U.S., the Sojourners community, the Catholic Worker movement, Pax Christi, the American Friends Service Committee, the War Resisters League, the Pledge of Resistance, and the Plowshares movement are actively promoting this nonviolent transformation. International Pax Christi (the International Catholic movement for peace), the International Fellowship of Reconciliation, Witness for Peace, and Latin America's Servicio Paz y Justicia are just a few of the signs of hope and light shining around the world at this very moment.

To deepen our commitment to active love and peaceful resistance, some are professing a vow of nonviolence. This choice of committed nonviolence is a way to help us remember the foundation on which we were created, to channel our energy to do what God wants. The vow helps us to love others wholeheartedly, to serve suffering humanity, to resist systemic violence—even to accept suffering rather than inflict it as we work for justice and peace. To transform the systems and cultures of violence into a new humanity of nonviolence, many of us are committing ourselves to the process of becoming sober. We are promising to become nonviolent and we are dedicating our lives to that process.

Committing Ourselves to Nonviolence for the Long Haul

Besides the great need for great love in our time, there are many other personal, practical reasons why a person may consider professing a vow of nonviolence. The vow may be psychologically helpful and supportive in a world which does not actively promote nonviolence. The vow can provide an individual with an anchor to hold fast to God. The vow can encapsulate the commitment to perpetual nonviolence in our being, behavior, attitude, and actions. Vowed nonviolence may become a new channel for the Spirit of God to work through God's people.

When we are tempted to use violence, a vow of nonviolence may become the instrument which holds us to the way of love. For example, a person vowed to nonviolence may be able to insist on nonviolence even when confronted by people of the third world who struggle to survive oppression and who take up arms and start killing.

A group of nonviolent demonstrators opposing the work of a nuclear weapons facility—though tempted to respond violently to workers, police officers, or counter-demonstrators—may have the strength to maintain their spirit of nonviolence. In a personal attack, mugging, threat, or arrest, we may be able to respond creatively and nonviolently because of a deep spiritual commitment to nonviolence.

In the moment of temptation when violence seems the best response, we can return to our vow of nonviolence, saying, "I vowed myself to accept and live out God's way of peace and active love. In this confrontation, I will not go back on my decision. I will resist violence through love, forgiveness, and my own willingness to take on suffering rather than inflicting it as I insist on human dignity and justice."

A vow of nonviolence may encourage faithfulness in difficult situations by inspiring faith in a God who may appear absent. A person vowed to nonviolence will be unable to take part in or support any violence, on any level, in any form. Those of us committed to nonviolence will train ourselves to respond to violence with loving nonviolence. Then if a violent assault should occur, our natural response will be active nonviolence.

Indeed, persons vowed to nonviolence will dedicate ourselves to experimenting with nonviolence. We will place ourselves in situations of violence to transform them with God's way of nonviolent love. We will know that the God of nonviolence will not abandon us but will be there in the moment of need.

A vow of nonviolence will encourage us to remain steadfast, saying, "I will not partake in the threat of violence or oppression. I will oppose violence actively and dramatically with all my being. I will cultivate a spirit of love and truth in my heart and be faithful to the commands of my God. I will participate in nonviolent transformation of the world."

The people who joined Francis of Assisi in his Third Order pledged never to carry or use weapons or to take the oath of fealty. These steps led eventually, according to historians, to the downfall of feudalism and fratricidal wars. Gandhi led his co-workers in a vow of nonviolence which helped his liberation campaigns change the history of the world.

In our own time, Martin Luther King, Jr., understood the importance of a serious commitment to nonviolence. In his campaign for civil rights in Birmingham, Alabama, in 1963, each participant was required to sign a commitment card which made the following promise of nonviolence.

I hereby pledge myself—my person and my body—to the nonviolent movement. Therefore, I will keep the following ten commandments:

1. Meditate daily on the teachings and life of Jesus.
2. Remember always that the nonviolent movement in Birmingham seeks justice and reconciliation—not victory.
3. Walk and talk in the manner of love, for God is love.
4. Pray daily to be used by God in order that all men and women might be free.

5. Sacrifice personal wishes in order that all men and women might be free.
6. Observe with both friend and foe the ordinary rules of courtesy.
7. Seek to perform regular service for others and for the world.
8. Refrain from the violence of fist, tongue, or heart.
9. Strive to be in good spiritual and bodily health.
10. Follow the directions of the movement and of the captain on a demonstration.

I sign this pledge, having seriously considered what I do and with the determination and will to persevere.[17]

King spent his life pleading the case for nonviolence as a way of social change for justice and peace. Our non-violent action needs to be free of any hate or violence within us. While he insisted that we hate injustice, King was convinced that hatred and violence toward others, especially in the movement for justice and peace, were useless and detrimental. King sought to make friends of enemies, to reconcile with opponents, and to build new relationships with all people based on the love of God. He understood the importance of a serious commitment to nonviolence. King knew that it was inconsistent to be non-violent in one area of our lives and violent in another. He wanted us to be disarmed by God so we could live in a dis-armed, nonviolent world.

A vow of nonviolence can be the new beginning of a life of experimentation and practice with nonviolence. It can provide a spiritual framework for living. The vow can also be a check against conformity to the violence of the status quo. The vow may sting our conscience and call us to be more loving, humble, truthful, provocative, public, and politically dangerous. Instead of worrying about the effectiveness of our life and actions, a vow of nonviolence may encourage us to persevere in the journey.

Vowing nonviolence can be a new channel of grace for our community. The public profession of a vow may help spark conversion and renewal in others, transform communal institutions and structures, and increase the love and commitment in one's community. A public profession of perpetual nonviolence may inspire others to a stronger commitment to God. It may stimulate dialogue, be a sign of hope, and witness to another way of life. Vowed nonviolence by many individuals may give birth to communities of nonviolence all over the world.

The vow of nonviolence is a gift from God; an alternative way of living in a world addicted to violence; a channel of renewal, reform, and refreshment; and a life-giving means of finding meaning and purpose in an age where the meaning of life is unclear and despair pervades. As an evangelical vow, it commits us to a specific life mission—transforming the world's addiction from violence into the sobriety of nonviolence.

Our great love for our suffering sisters and brothers may inspire us also to profess wholehearted nonviolence. We pledge nonviolence because we love the entire human family and long never to harm anyone.

Finally, we profess a vow of nonviolence not just because we love all suffering humanity—a love which is really quite imperfect—*but because God loves suffering humanity*, because God loves the whole human family *unconditionally*. A person who receives and accepts this tremendous love of God can witness to it by publicly adhering to this love through a vow of nonviolence.

Theologian John Howard Yoder puts it this way:

> The reason for the Christian's being called to live above this world's battles is not that one of the Ten Commandments enjoins us not to kill, or not that Jesus as a new lawgiver or-

ders us to love our enemies. The Christian has been disarmed by God. There is no need for orders to love one's neighbors, beginning in the smallest circle of daily relationships, or one's enemies; the Christian is driven to this by the love of Christ within his or her life.[18]

The vow of nonviolence is not an order or a law we place over ourselves. Instead, *the vow of nonviolence is a way of witnessing to others that God has disarmed us and wants to disarm us all.*

The vow of nonviolence is *a recognition of who we are*—a disarmed, nonviolent people, who have been and are continually being disarmed by the God of nonviolence. God is making our hearts nonviolent, forming us into the image of the nonviolent Christ. The vow accepts this work of God and witnesses to God's Spirit of nonviolence as a new way of life. A vow of nonviolence may help us to love greatly in time of great need and thus further the disarmament of hearts and nations.

5

The Vow of Nonviolence: A Pledge of Peaceful Resistance and Active Love

THE vow of nonviolence can be a channel for God's grace of nonviolence to work in our hearts and lives. It can be an instrument of God's nonviolent revolution that transforms our hearts and frees us to live new lives of peacemaking. For the Christian, this vow can be a new expression of the baptismal vow. It can renew the public witness made at baptism. The vow can be a formal acceptance of what God has done in our lives. It can help us to live out that gift of nonviolent action.

Living Out Our Baptismal Promises

To understand the vow of nonviolence, let us examine the Christian baptismal promises and the regular renewal of those promises. The early Christians called the baptismal initiation into the Christian faith a "sacrament" because they understood the political and social implications of baptism. They knew that in an empire of violence which demanded allegiance to the emperor as a god, profession of faith to the living God and God's Christ would be understood as treason and result in execution. Many early Christians were martyred immediately after their baptism.

The word "sacrament," which today means a sign or symbol of something sacred, was adopted by the early Christians from the Latin word *sacramentum*, which referred to an oath of allegiance made by soldiers to their commander and the imperial gods of Rome.[1] This *sacramentum* involved a religious ceremony in a sacred place and committed the soldier to lifelong obedience to the imperial god.

Christian writers in the second century borrowed the term *sacramentum* to explain to their Roman contemporaries what the ceremony of Christian initiation was all about. Baptism, they said, was something like the *sacramentum* administered to new recruits of the Roman army. It was a ritual through which people began a new life of service and allegiance to God and God's nonviolent way of life.[2]

Today Christian baptism is hardly a threat to empires and the systems of injustice that kill people. It does not connote the strict allegiance to Christian nonviolence and resistance to imperial violence implicit in early Christianity. A vow of nonviolence tries to take us back to that early witness and lifestyle of Christian nonviolence. It formally commits us to the way of nonviolence which was at the core of baptism and Christian initiation in the first few centuries.

Today's baptismal promises renounce sin and profess faith in God and the good news of Jesus Christ. The promises admit a person into a new covenant of love with God. They accept God and mark a new beginning to live out this gift of faith and to witness to what God has done.

The annual renewal of baptismal promises at Easter begins with a series of questions and affirmations which reveal what God has done in us and how we will continue to accept God's loving action. At the Easter renewal, the presider begins with the invitation, "Now that we have completed our Lenten observance, let us renew the promises we made in baptism when we rejected Satan and his works and promised to serve God faithfully. Do you reject sin so as to live in the freedom of God's children?"

Each person then responds, "I do."

"Do you reject the glamour of evil and refuse to be mastered by sin?"

"I do."

"Do you reject Satan, father of sin and prince of darkness?"

"I do."

"Do you believe in God the Creator of heaven and earth?"

"I do."

"Do you believe in Jesus Christ, who was born of Mary, was crucified, died and was buried, rose from the dead, and is now seated at the right hand of God?"

"I do."

"Do you believe in the Holy Spirit, the forgiveness of sins, the resurrection of the body and life everlasting?"

"I do."

The presider concludes, "The God of Jesus Christ has given us a new birth by water and the Holy Spirit, forgiven all our sins, and made us into God's sons and daughters. May God also keep us faithful to Jesus Christ for ever and ever."

Everyone responds, "Amen."[3]

Part of the Catholic rite of Christian initiation includes renouncing false worship. In one formula, the presider asks a significant question: "Christ Jesus alone has the power to protect men and women. Are you determined never to abandon Jesus and return to the use of N.?"

In place of "N," the presider "names objects which are used superstitiously or other ways of defense which deny the lordship of Christ."

Given our world's addiction to violence, today we could easily place the words "violence," "war" or "nuclear weapons" in that question to point to the false idols which have taken precedence over our true allegiance to God and to Christ.

The vow of nonviolence can be a sign of new commitment to the Christian way of life which rejects the ways of violence and dependence on weapons of violence and embraces the way of nonviolence and dependence on God. A vow of nonviolence may be a new form of renewal and confirmation into the Christian faith, a new rite of initiation like baptismal promises.

The vow may formally commit the Christian to Christ's way of nonviolence, a way not often emphasized, discussed, preached, or practiced by today's Christians. The vow of nonviolence is not an expression of one's unique calling within the Christian community but an expression of one's calling to be a Christian.

The vow may make explicit what godparents once promised for us at our baptism. It may be an explication of our baptismal commitment and thus a help to live the Christian life. It can be seen as a new baptismal commitment for Christians because, like the baptismal renewals, it rejects Satan—who is implicated in all the violence in the world.

The vow embraces Christ, the incarnation of nonviolence, and Christ's new life of peacemaking solidarity with the poor, resistance to systemic injustice, and evangelical nonviolence. The vow of nonviolence is the explicit rejection of the idols which have defended us such as Trident submarines or cruise missiles. The vow declares that we no longer worship the false gods of violence but trust in God and will try to follow God's way of peace through suffering active love.

The vow of nonviolence makes explicit what is implicit in the baptismal vow. It helps renew our baptism into Christianity. The vow does not create a new insight into Christianity but professes to the world and specifically to the Christian community that to be a Christian is to be nonviolent.

The person pledging nonviolence acknowledges the receipt of new grace of nonviolence in her Christian life and makes a formal pledge of acceptance. This acceptance demands an active response. The real power and commitment of the vow lies in the fact that one can no longer say, "I did not know this graced way of nonviolence existed." Once we accept the grace of nonviolence, we are called a life committed to nonviolence.

The vow of nonviolence is public recognition of change in a person, the recognition of who that person is and who we are all called to be. Through the vow we accept the gift of a lifetime of nonviolence. The vowed life of nonviolence becomes a free choice that we accept and choose openly, wholeheartedly, continually, to the degree that we are open to God's grace. The vow can be the formal beginning of a lifelong, public experiment in truth and love, as well as a shield in times of frustration, hopelessness, and failure.

The vow of nonviolence witnesses to the presence of God's reign in our hearts and our world. It vows allegiance to Jesus Christ, to his nonviolent way of life and to God's reign of nonviolent love. It can renew our Christianity and draw it more in line with the witness of the early church and its martyrs of nonviolence.

The Risky Life of Vowed Nonviolence

The vow of nonviolence moves us from comfortable complacency into the dangerous, risky way of nonviolence. The life of vowed nonviolence gets us back to the roots of our faith. It leads to constant conversion and deeper union with God.

Thomas Merton wrote that nonviolence is "nothing more than a living out of a nonviolence of the heart, an inner unity already experienced in prayer." [4] Active nonviolence flows from a disarmed heart with the truth that the unity already realized inside of us is also present in all humanity. It is a sharing of the disarmament, the unity, and the love that is overflowing in our hearts. It signals a spiritual explosion of nonviolence occurring within us. It understands that all human beings are one and so manifests compassion and forgiveness in thought, word, and deed toward all.

A vow of nonviolence can mark the beginning of a life of experimenting in truth (as Gandhi described his life). It can help us take another step of accompaniment with the poor and marginalized of the world, to walk with them as they pursue Christ's reign of justice and peace here and now. The vow of nonviolence is the prayerful pledge made in freedom to do what is right no matter how hopeless a situation or life itself may appear. "The soul of peacemaking is the will to give one's life," Daniel Berrigan writes.[5]

"The truest act of courage, the strongest act of humanity is to sacrifice ourselves for others in a totally nonviolent struggle for justice," Cesar Chavez declares.[6] The willingness to serve, suffer, and even die for God's nonviolent struggle of justice and peace is the pledge of vowed nonviolence. It marks an end of violence and a new beginning of God's nonviolence.

The Commitment of Vowed Nonviolence

The vow of nonviolence commits us more and more to God and thus to all humanity. We pledge not to harm others ever again and promise to withdraw our consent from the world's systemic violence. We declare that we will try to avoid every possible manifestation of violence, from inflicting physical injury or death on others, to participating in national or international violence, to practicing verbal abuse, psychological manipulation, dishonesty, greed, or hatred (even in the privacy of our hearts).

By abstaining from violence, the vow offers a life of active nonviolence, a commitment to love everyone everywhere on all fronts. But even more, our vow pledges peaceful resistance to every form of injustice and systemic violence. The vow of nonviolence sets free Christ's Spirit of active love and peaceful resistance in our lives and into the public arena of the world's violence.

Preparation for the Vow of Nonviolence

The vow of nonviolence may best be professed in community, with the support of friends who are also trying to live nonviolent lives. We can prepare for this commitment by asking God to open our minds and disarm our hearts.

We can study and meditate on the Scriptures from the perspective of active nonviolence and the perspective of the oppressed and marginalized peoples of the world. We can examine our own addiction to violence. We can study the realities of violence in our world as well as the lives and writings of the practitioners of nonviolence, such as Gandhi, Martin Luther King, Jr., Dorothy Day, Thomas Merton, Oscar Romero, Jean Donovan, Ita Ford, Jim Douglass, Daniel Berrigan, and others. Most important, we can prepare by following the lead of God's Spirit and experimenting with nonviolence right now, wherever we are.

We can profess the vow of nonviolence suggested by

Pax Christi (at the beginning of the book) or write our own, perhaps including these ingredients: "Before God and the human family, I vow myself to God's way of non-violence. I vow to practice Jesus' way of active love and peaceful resistance to evil, to seek truth and justice all my life, to witness to God's nonviolent reign of justice and peace. I vow to cooperate with God's Spirit of reconciliation, love, justice, and peace, in my own heart and mind, in all my relationships, and in the world. Thus I will follow in the steps of Jesus Christ, the way of nonviolence."

The nonviolent life in all its fullness can be adopted and embraced by any human being who desires to live nonviolently, who hears the call of God to a deeper commitment of truth and love. Young people, old people, church people, ministers, priests, nuns, religious men and women, communities—all Christians can consider making the life commitment of vowed nonviolence. A vow of nonviolence might be professed by married couples to help them become more nonviolent with each other and their children; to help them fulfill their life commitment; and to help them live as a sign of God's nonviolent love to each other, their children, and the world.

The vow of nonviolence is a real option for all who want to commit their lives to God and to humanity. It can be professed by those already working against systems of violence. It may inspire a deeper search into nonviolence. For those already actively involved and deeply committed to the lifelong struggle for justice and peace, it may inspire a renewal of nonviolence and help maintain a nonviolent spirit in the struggle. The vow of nonviolence may be helpful to those who have spent many years in the work of resistance to violence and are sorely tempted to succumb to the spirit of violence in frustration and despair.

After prayerful discernment, a vow of nonviolence can be especially helpful and meaningful to someone who has recently undergone a conversion—for example, a convert to the faith. With a vow, people can pledge themselves explicitly to Christ's way of nonviolence as they embark on a new life of discipleship.

Persons who have made careers working for the military or have helped design nuclear weapons or have spent lives in the greedy pursuit of money may leave their jobs in an effort to follow God's will and fit their lives into the vision of the gospel. Such people may be helped by a vow of nonviolence as they start new lives of service, nonviolence, love, resistance, forgiveness, and transformation.

The vow can help us persevere in our new commitment, especially as we suffer the misunderstanding of our family and friends who disagree with our heartfelt anti-nuclear, anti-violence work. In an effort to remain nonviolent, those working in places of persecution and war where people are suffering and killing one another daily may find it helpful to vow nonviolence as a way to stay centered in the nonviolent life of Christ.

The vow of nonviolence accepts the gift God has given to us and publicly witnesses to the reality of nonviolence. This vow may help us to be faithful to God's covenant of love and peace, to become God's sons and daughters, to be a new people of nonviolence.

In an age when so much has been lost because of our addiction to violence and death, a vow of nonviolence may help us to live soberly, to renounce violence, and to remain strong and firm in the life of nonviolence. But this new commitment to God's way of nonviolence will have consequences. The consequences and implications for this life of nonviolence need to be faced squarely as we consider professing a vow of nonviolence.

6

Implications for the Life of Vowed Nonviolence

LESS than one year after professing a vow of nonviolence, I was led to work in a soup kitchen and a shelter for the homeless in New York City, then to a refugee camp for a few months in El Salvador, and finally into a jail cell for prayerful, nonviolent civil disobedience to the nuclear arms race. In all these places my convictions were tested.

Subsequently I worked in a shelter and drop-in center for the homeless in inner-city Washington, D.C., and traveled extensively into the war zones of Central America, Haiti, and the Philippines. I dedicated myself to nonviolent campaigns to stop U.S. military aid to El Salvador, end nuclear weapons testing, and resist the U.S. war in the Persian Gulf.

My life of active nonviolence took me across the country, to military bases and nuclear installations, to speak out and act publicly for God's nonviolent reign of justice and peace. I have been arrested and jailed many times. The choice I made to embrace the nonviolent way of life has influenced my life decisions and my responses to the world's wars and violence. The vow of nonviolence, I discovered, has consequences.

As a response to God's call and as a way of life, the vow of nonviolence entails many lifelong implications which will shape our lives and deepen throughout the rest of our lives. A vow of nonviolence can lay the foundation, the formal groundwork, for a life of spontaneous, Spirit-filled nonviolence.

The vow can help set the stage and form the spiritual attitude of our lives so that we may be more open to God's disarming action and nonviolence in our lives. It can prepare us to respond with creative nonviolence to the situations of our daily lives and to the violence of our world. The vow makes explicit what is implicit in our hearts, that God is transforming us into instruments of God's nonviolent love. The vow signals that we have been born again in the way of nonviolence, that our lives now reflect the peacemaking life of the nonviolent Jesus.

This pledge to witness to God's great gift of Jesus Christ and the good news of his nonviolence will have specific implications and ramifications. A look at the many characteristics of a life of vowed nonviolence will help us understand God's way of nonviolence and the new life we are called to live.

The characteristics of lifelong nonviolence are inherent to every Christian's discipleship, for one cannot be faithful to Christ without adopting Christ's nonviolence and trying to be nonviolent like Christ. The vow of nonviolence formally commits us to this mandate of the gospel. The vow proclaims to the Christian community and to the whole world the gift of peace that God offers to us all.

A Commitment to Unconditional Love and Active Compassion

The vow of nonviolence commits us to the daily practice and pursuit of active, spiritual nonviolence. The active love of *agape* and the steadfast search for truth take the forefront of our new life in nonviolence. The vow commits us to try to love ourselves, others, our enemies, the poor, and all people unconditionally and sacrificially, without personal gain, for the rest of our lives.

This love includes an active willingness to take on suffering and violence without retaliating. It invites us to serve others, especially the poor and marginalized, without desiring service in return.

Compassion is a good word to describe the fundamental attitude and lifestyle of *agape*. Compassion is that active love which sides with all those who suffer from violence. *Compassion* means to "suffer with." It sums up the basic attitude which we try to cultivate and practice in a life vowed to God's nonviolence.

When Jesus spoke of being "compassionate" and "perfect" as God is "compassionate" and "perfect" (Matt. 5:48), he summed up the fullness of the nonviolent life. The compassionate heart recognizes the shared humanity in every person—oppressor or oppressed. It understands the brokenness in everyone, in all those who suffer from violence and who commit violence.

Compassion sides with the oppressed and actively invites everyone's transformation into nonviolence. It sees every human being as a child of God and relates to every human being as a brother or a sister. The compassionate heart has a burning desire to help heal all who suffer from oppression. It befriends the poor and marginalized and transforms us so that we join their ranks, perhaps by landing us in jail and prison for nonviolent resistance to systemic violence.

Vowed Nonviolence Means
Active Resistance to Evil

The vow is a commitment to resist systemic injustice without using violence. The nonviolent person who maintains heartfelt love for all people will renounce not only active but passive aggression, which is a more subtle and sometimes a more destructive form of hostility.

A person vowed to nonviolence takes up Gandhi's challenge "to lay down our lives for what we consider to be right." [1] Hatred, bitterness, or revenge find no place in such steadfast opposition to violence. Instead, the possibility of conversion, transformation, and reconciliation are relentlessly pursued. In our nonviolent resistance, such vowed nonviolence declares, "I am so determined to right this injustice that I am willing to suffer and die to bring about God's nonviolent transformation of justice and peace."

Nonviolence does not resort to the more common and less effective reasoning which says, "I am so determined to right this injustice that I am going to make my opponent suffer for it and may even kill my opponent to bring about what I see as right." [2] According to the logic of nonviolence, such a willingness to accept and absorb suffering in the struggle for justice and peace will open the eyes of those who inflict violence and oppress others until they see what they are doing and whom they are killing. This awakening is the process of nonviolent transformation to which we commit ourselves in the vow of nonviolence.

In an age of nuclear weapons, systemic injustice, and warfare, faithfulness to a vow of nonviolence will likely lead to prayerful, nonviolent civil disobedience. In a world addicted to violence and threatened with global destruction, those vowed to nonviolence will find it necessary at some point to cross the line from legal opposition to institutionalized violence to that illegal peacemaking of nonviolent direct action which risks arrest and prison for the witness of peace. Our fidelity to the God of nonviolence may lead us, like Jesus, to arrest, jail, trial, torture, and even death.

Preparation for nonviolent civil disobedience will include prayer, discernment, communal discussion, role-playing, and training in nonviolent response. Our preparation yields a loving, disarmed heart that seeks to disarm others, even those who support systemic violence and imprison us. Our civil disobedience will develop as a natural consequence and proper step along the journey of nonviolence.

Nonviolent civil disobedience is a way to accept suffering while struggling for justice in the world. It can help prick the conscience of the world and shake us out of our apathy and complicity in systemic violence. Such illegal direct action confronts the laws which legalize and defend the world's addiction to violence, including the nuclear weapons which threaten to destroy us all.

A Commitment to Truth

Nonviolence by its very nature invites a steadfast search for truth and a meticulous adherence to truth. Gandhi coined a new word, *satyagraha*, to describe the process of truth-seeking. *Satyagraha* means "holding on to truth," or "truth force." Gandhi characterized the nonviolent person, not just as one who abstains from violence, but as a *satyagrahi*, "one who holds on to truth." [3]

Our lives should be centered in truth, Gandhi suggested. Truth should be the breath of our life, he said. In the wholehearted search for truth, we may only glimpse its fullness now and then. Yet we are called to uphold the vision of truth as best we can. This pursuit of truth can only be practiced, he insisted, through nonviolence. We cannot insist on what we see as the truth by hurting or killing others because that denies the very ground of truth, the truthful reality that they are our sisters and brothers.

A commitment to the truth acts in the truth and in the spirit of nonviolence. One pursues justice and peace because it is truthful, because it is the right thing to do. As we journey along the path of nonviolence into truth, we willingly change and accept further revelation of truth. This requires the utmost respect for other individuals who cling to their glimpse of truth; it requires a willingness to dialogue and seek compromise. It demands a persistent and focused effort to incarnate and realize truth in the present.

For Gandhi, truth was the end to be fully realized and nonviolence was the means to that end. A steadfast commitment to truth is realized through a life of loving nonviolence and resistance to all that is not true, beginning with the lie of violence and war. The vow of nonviolence calls us to be honest. The person vowed to nonviolence strives never to tell a lie or to participate in lies. Our vow calls us to speak out against the global lie which denies that we are addicted to violence, that there is no other alternative to war and nuclear weapons, that violence is justified. A life of nonviolence is a life of speaking truth publicly and accepting the consequences of our truth-telling.

A Life of Prayer and Contemplation

The life of nonviolence and truth requires a living faith in the God of nonviolence and truth. Since the person of nonviolence seeks truth, understands truth as God, and knows God as truth-full, this person commits herself to finding God's truth.

Prayer is the best way to seek out the truth of reality and to live the truth of nonviolence. "Nonviolence is not an easy thing to understand, still less to practice, weak as we are," Gandhi wrote. "We must all act prayerfully and humbly and continually ask God to open the eyes of our understanding, being ever ready to act according to the light as we daily receive it." [4]

The life vowed to nonviolence is rooted in prayer. It is a life that turns in prayer daily to the God of nonviolence for grace and strength to live faithfully. The first and last act every day for the nonviolent person is an act of prayer. This life of prayer will disarm us, bear fruit, and lead to nonviolent action. The nonviolent life thus includes the necessary ingredients of daily prayer, meditation, silence, solitude, and contemplation of the God of nonviolence.

Prayer is daily communication with God. It means listening to God, talking with God, and experiencing the presence of God in our lives. Such prayer takes time. It demands a priority in our lives. It requires solitude and faithful dedication. Prayer is the development of our relationship with God. Without an ongoing relationship with the God of peace, our nonviolence will be meaningless and passive; it will ultimately give way to despair and violence. The God of our prayer who disarms us is the motivating force behind all our nonviolence. "Prayer is most fundamentally a covenantal relationship with another person—God—and it partakes of all the risks, struggles, joys, and darknesses that attach to any personal intimacy," writes John Kavanaugh.[5]

As we enter more fully into awareness of our relationship with God, we become aware that God's Spirit is leading us. Daily discernment and especially the help of a spiritual director can reveal which spirit is of God, rooted in God's nonviolent love—and which spirit is not of God but rooted in violence. God whispers her desires for active nonviolence to us as we prayerfully listen, dialogue, and act nonviolently.

The nonviolent life discerns that inner still voice that moves us to love and nonviolence. Our nonviolent action becomes a response to God's action in our lives. In our life of prayer we come, not merely to know about God, but to know God personally as our friend, confidant, parent, lover, and significant other.

This intimate relationship with God grows and develops throughout our life and becomes deeper than any other relationship. As we grow in love with God, we discover that we are the beloved sons and daughters of God. We remember that every person is our sister and brother, all life is sacred, and we are all called to become people of God's nonviolence.

Prayer begins with a recognition of our own violence, a confession of sin, an admission that we too are addicted to violence. As Twelve Step programs teach, from this recognition of our powerlessness in the face of addiction, we turn to God, the Higher Power, and ask for help. In the life of prayer, we turn to God to help us all become people of nonviolence.

As we listen to and are disarmed by God, we ask God to disarm our sisters and brothers and bring about God's reign of nonviolence in our world. Our life of prayer may lead us to fast and repent. It will open our hearts so God can love through us as we reach out in love to our enemies.

Prayer helps us to live more fully in the present moment and to become transparent so that the God of peace shines through us. Our lives of nonviolence will mature through prayer which helps us to recognize our limitations and weakness before God.

A vow of nonviolence is a commitment to give our hearts to God and thus to suffering humanity. Through our vow we promise to seek first God's reign of justice and peace, beginning with our own hearts and then in the world. In a world of violence and injustice, the life of prayer is subversive and revolutionary.

The daily prayer of lifelong nonviolence will root all our actions in God. By opening ourselves to do what God wants, our acts will originate from God and be accompanied by peace in the very depths of our beings.

The Nonviolent Heart Trusts in the God of Nonviolence

The person vowed to nonviolence does not worship nonviolence but God. The life vowed to nonviolence searches for God in the quiet of one's heart and in the chaos of the world. Our prayerful search for truth, nonviolence, and God will lead us to let go more easily of our own agendas and trust more fully in God.

The vow of nonviolence can lead us to seek God as Gandhi sought God—through the way of active nonviolence. "What I want to achieve, what I have been striving and pining to achieve all these years is self-realization, to see God face to face," Gandhi wrote in his autobiography.

> I live and move and have my being in pursuit of this goal. All that I do by way of speaking and writing, and all my ventures in the political field, are directed to this same end. . . . I have not yet found God but I am seeking after God. I am prepared to sacrifice things dearest to me in pursuit of this quest. Even if that sacrifice demanded be my very life, I hope I may be prepared to give it. . . . God alone is real and all else is unreal." [6]

As we seek truth, we will humbly and boldly witness to what we see as right and true. With respect, concern, and love for others, we will publicly object to the denial of truth, even when it is dangerous, scandalous, and risky to do so. We will testify to the truth of God as we have come to understand it.

Trust in God and commitment to love and truth will free us from fear. Fear is the opposite of love and a root cause of violence. Gandhi wrote that fearlessness is a prerequisite of nonviolence. We enter into God's nonviolence when we let go of all our fears and trust in God. In a life vowed to the way of nonviolence, God invites us not to fear anyone or anything.

The grace of fearlessness is one of the first fruits of nonviolence. It is a gift from God. As we act nonviolently in the world, we learn to trust in God so thoroughly that, like Gandhi, King, Ford, or the Jesuit martyrs of El Salvador, we can stand up even to the forces of death. Our violent world is plagued with fear. We all fear rejection, abandonment, denial, betrayal, loneliness, embarrassment, arrest, imprisonment, pain, and torture. Fear can paralyze us and prevent us from walking the way of nonviolence. God invites us to stop being paralyzed by our fears and walk.

Our greatest fear is the fear of death. The way of nonviolence invites us to see death as an entrance into eternal life with God. Our lifelong nonviolence will inspire us with such faith, trust, hope, and dependence on God that even fear of death will vanish. Our practice of nonviolence will take us so close to the forces of violence and death in our world that we will no longer perceive death as a threat but as a deeper entrance into the unconditional, nonviolent love of God.

As we accompany the poor and the marginalized who daily face the possibility of death, we too will face the constant reality of death. As we place our lives in God's hands we can be free from the fear of death.

This life of nonviolence will free us from fear so we can live in the joyful presence of the God who raised Jesus from the dead. As we become more aware of God's presence in our lives and feel the risen Jesus living in us, we will live each day as if it were our last on earth. Our lives then will become more rooted in God, centered on God, and open to loving every person we encounter.

We will prepare for death. We will be ready to die in a spirit of nonviolence, to forgive those who kill us, to find meaning in death, and to hand over our lives to God. In the face of violence, the nonviolent person will seek to remain calm and unafraid, to maintain dialogue and eye contact and act in God's Spirit of nonviolent love.

As we delve into nonviolence, we will name our fears, share them with each other, put them behind us, and move into the nonviolence of God. A deep trust in God will give us the courage to act beyond our fear, to believe that God supports us, and to know that God will transform everything into God's reign. As we let go of fear and begin to trust in God, we will let go of our anxieties and seek only God.

As we place greater faith and trust in God, we find courage to stand up and resist injustice through nonviolence. When physical violence is possible, we need to be prepared to respond without threatening or intimidating others. This fearless commitment to human life seeks to free those who do violence and support injustice by calling forth the love inside them so that they can be the people they truly wish to be. Such courage recognizes the humanity in everyone and reaches out in love to even the most violent people.

The Powerful Powerlessness of Nonviolence

Through the vow of nonviolence, God will lead us deeper and deeper into God's own powerful powerlessness—the powerlessness of the poor. Nonviolence renounces the coercive power of violence and the dominating power of control and instead enters into the powerlessness of the poor. It offers solidarity with those who have no control over their lives, such as the starving children of the world.

By vowing nonviolence, we renounce the domination

and control of violence and hand over control of our lives to God. To be nonviolent in today's world is to let go of power. Nonviolence shuns coercive power and has nothing to do with the power of violence. It accepts powerlessness and lets God act through our weakness. As we accept the powerful powerlessness of God, we become more vulnerable and thus more nonviolent. We place our security not in violence, intimidation, control, weapons, or possession, but in God.

Such powerlessness does not mean that we participate in and support violence. Our powerlessness breaks the spiral of violence. A wife abused by her violent husband, for example, should nonviolently break that cycle of violence by leaving him and encouraging him to get help. The powerlessness of nonviolence, however, would not allow her to kill her husband but to nonviolently resist him. Powerlessness is thus another way of saying that we will not kill people or retaliate with violence. Instead, we will respond creatively, through the powerless power of nonviolence.

As we enter into solidarity with the poor and the powerless, we live out our vow of nonviolence by voluntarily becoming poor, renouncing our possessions, and siding with those who have nothing. The vow of nonviolence is a commitment to enter the world of the poor. Though this is nearly impossible for white middle-class North American men like me, we are all still called to move in that direction.

We simplify our lifestyles, choose to live among the poor and marginalized, and walk with those who are oppressed. For North Americans, such active nonviolence will be scandalous, but it will proclaim the seriousness of our commitment and the reality of God's presence in our lives. In this life of solidarity with the poor, we accompany our friends in their suffering and powerlessness and struggle with them for justice and peace.

As we do, we will be transformed by them and by the God of the poor. Our friends will teach us what it means to be nonviolent, to trust in God. They will offer us hope. A life of solidarity with the poor and oppressed is the best expression of nonviolence because it deals with the realities of systemic violence. The witness of nonviolence in North America is a lifestyle of solidarity with the poor that resists systemic violence and speaks to the powers that be about God's justice and peace.

To reject violence is to renounce our possessions so we will have nothing to defend and no reason to hurt anyone. The involuntary poverty of destitution is the worst form of violence. The possessions we own and do not need belong to the poor, from whom we have in effect stolen what we own. To resist structures that kill and oppress the poor, we remove ourselves as much as possible from the wealth and benefits of those structures. As we live with the poor, we become more hospitable and learn from the poor to share our hearts and lives with everyone.

Through voluntary poverty and powerlessness, we learn to recognize our own weakness, to understand the depth of our spiritual poverty, and to rely more on God for everything. Such vulnerability and powerlessness does not mean passivity but refuses to resort to the false security of violence and the luxury of despair. As we live out our spiritual and physical poverty, we will grow in the riches of God. In our powerlessness, we let go of any sense of accomplishment, any inkling of control, and all concern for effectiveness.

Instead we rely on God and concentrate on the beauty of God's nonviolence, justice, and peace. We trust in God to bring about reconciliation, knowing that we are powerless in the face of the world's addiction to violence. Our life experiences testify to the truth that God alone can transform us. When nonviolence appears to result in failure, frustration, discomfort, dissatisfaction, and loss, the person of nonviolence continues to trust in God. In our powerlessness, we may then approach even greater solidarity with the poor and the powerless of the world.

In this solidarity we focus on the truth. We do what is right, abandon all control, and leave the results to God since this is what God has asked of us. Our shared powerlessness with the poor in the nonviolent struggle for justice will reveal our shared humanity and help us all to know that we are God's sons and daughters.

As we empty ourselves for the cause of nonviolence, we can trust that everything we do can tap into the love of God. As we let go of greed, possessions, money, honor, and pride, and concentrate on God, we will be emptied and then filled with the Spirit of God's nonviolent love. Our lives will be out of our control and in God's hands. Though we possess few things, like the poor and oppressed of the world, our hearts will be filled with God's spirit of peace and love.

In this life of powerlessness, we are called to chastity, whether of spirit only or body as well, whether as single people, married people, or consecrated celibates. The vow of nonviolence pledges our hearts to God and to suffering humanity. Thus, we are called to a deep reverence of human life, to God's gift of human sexuality, and to human dignity. We are drawn away from anything that is violent or could hurt others. We try to cultivate and choose a purity of heart which is also a purity of body, mind, soul, and spirit. The practice of chastity will free us for a deeper, more intimate love of God and thus a more intimate love for all humanity.

Linked to this life of powerlessness is a spirit of humility. We remember that we are weak human beings, created from the dust of the earth, as the Scripture says. We let go of selfish desires and enter the hidden, humble life of the poor who trust in God. The humble heart does not compete or get caught up in comparison but rests in a basic trust in God and a love for all people. Rooted in envy and pride, the competitive spirit which seeks the assertion of the ego is abandoned as another trick of violence. Active nonviolence reflects instead a spirit of contrition, humility, and invitation. The nonviolent quest is a journey into humility which abandons all self-interest and focuses on the interests of God and suffering humanity.

The disarmed heart recognizes its limitations, mistakes, and sinfulness through honest self-examination. It understands that God is God and manifests appropriate dignity and self-respect—but keeps the ego in place. A humble spirit recognizes its basic equality with all other human beings and rejects arrogance or superiority. The humble nonviolent person is inclusive and open toward all people and accepts the humiliation brought on by the scandal of nonviolence.

False humility is antithetical to the life of nonviolence. We cannot argue that we are too humble, too weak, or too sinful to get involved in the nonviolent struggle for justice. Real humility calls us to a life of active nonviolence, despite our sins and weaknesses because real humility keeps the focus on God. Likewise if we use our vow of nonviolence to promote ourselves, prove our dedicated superiority, or highlight our holiness, we contradict the very essence of our vow.

True humility transforms our poverty, our arrogance, our self-image, our self-righteousness, and any manipulative spirit that seeks approval or domination.[7] True humility constantly overturns our selfishness into active nonviolence that serves justice and peace.

Jim Wallis, editor of *Sojourners* magazine, pinpoints this commitment to humble love which is at the heart of our Christian nonviolence.

Whenever our protest becomes an effort to "prove ourselves," we are in serious danger. Our best actions are those which admit our complicity in the evil we protest and are marked by a spirit of genuine repentance and humility. Our worst actions are those which seek to demonstrate our own righteousness, our purity, our freedom from complicity. When our pride overtakes our protest, we may simply be repeating, in political form, the self-righteous judgment of the fundamentalists—"I'm saved, and you're not." . . . Although our actions we undertake will never substitute for grace, they can indeed be witnesses of God's grace. Since they lack the capacity to justify us, a better purpose for our actions would be to bear faithful witness.[8]

Nonviolence Is Always Willing to Forgive

The spirit of unconditional forgiveness is a fundamental mark of nonviolence. An attitude of mercy and compassion toward others will enable us to forgive others for hurting us, even to forgive those who would kill our friends, our family members, or ourselves. The merciful, forgiving heart strives to be so pure that it holds no trace of hatred, bitterness, anger, judgment, cynicism, or condemnation. Instead, it taps into the boundless compassion of God who forgives everyone.

The nonviolent person cultivates a spirit of gratitude and patient perseverance. The vow of nonviolence is a promise to forgive, to avoid judging or condemning others. Such mercy and forgiveness toward everyone still insists on the truth of justice and peace. It insists that reconciliation takes priority over pride. Mercy promotes reconciliation. Forgiveness leads to peace. Nonviolence is a way of practicing mercy and forgiveness so that reconciliation, peace, and justice become a reality.

"It has always been a mystery to me how people can feel themselves honored by the humiliation of their fellow human beings," Gandhi wrote in his autobiography.[9] Anything that humiliates another person breaks the human family and causes resentment, anger, hatred—and further violence. A vow of nonviolence invites us to use the transforming love of God to oppose the systems which humiliate and oppress people. The person vowed to nonviolence edifies other people with a spirit of mercy, forgiveness, love, and constant affirmation. In this way, we help people to see that we are all God's children.

The vow of nonviolence is a pledge to forgive everyone for everything. The vow works toward the day when everyone will learn to live in the peace of God's forgiveness. The person vowed to nonviolence does not seek justice as it is commonly perceived. When society speaks of "justice," it refers to punishment and retribution. Nonviolence does not punish; it transforms. Nonviolence promotes a change of heart, transforms the lives of those who commit violence, and sparks reconciliation between peoples.

To practice lifelong forgiveness, the person of nonviolence learns to control anger. Anger is not a sin; it is neutral. Anger is often channeled into violent retribution. Nonviolence channels anger into positive, peaceful action for justice. Anger directed at others or oneself can contribute to violence; it can eat away at the spirit of love and leave an empty shell of bitterness.

A life of anger can take away our joy. Anger toward others offends God and does not reflect God; God does not harbor anger, but overflows with love and mercy. The person vowed to nonviolence tries not to harbor anger at others, refuses to give in to the anger of others, tries not to retaliate in a spirit of violent anger, and seeks to transform the anger of others through love into a spirit of peace. One cannot be nonviolent, loving, and compassionate toward others and remain perpetually angry with them. Our anger needs to be acknowledged, accepted as part of our human life, and converted through prayer into a forgiving, nonviolent love.

Anger against injustice and violence, when not directed at people but at the works of evil, can be focused to energize us for the nonviolent struggle of justice. Anger toward injustice can renew commitment to justice and peace. The nonviolence of Jesus and Gandhi, however, is best practiced when rooted in a disarmed heart that overflows with love and peace.

An insistence on justice and truth that flows from love rather than anger is ultimately more godly. Certainly God has enough reason to be angry with us for all the destruction we have caused; instead, our God of unconditional love calls us to justice and peace. Such active nonviolence, rooted in this love and mercy, will lead us toward reconciliation.

Nonviolence Is Creative

If a person vowed to nonviolence is threatened with violence or is present when one person is harming another, then the person dedicated to nonviolence will immediately respond in a spirit of love with creative nonviolence that seeks to end the violence and disarm everyone. Such nonviolence believes that God will act through our nonviolent actions to transform every situation of violence into reconciliation and justice. Personal nonviolence extends even to such dramatic instances and demands courageous and active responses of love and trust in God.

The vowed nonviolent person will intervene and do everything possible short of violence to stop violence. Because nonviolence can take a thousand forms, such nonviolent action will be unique, creative, peaceful, wise, and confident. The nonviolent person who is mugged, for example, gives away any material goods that are asked for (if he or she has any), but will never give in to violence or submit to injustice, fear, intimidation, and oppression. Such a person will maintain a posture of love, dignity, mercy, and forgiveness; will continue to insist on the truth of our shared humanity; and will seek to disarm others with an open hand of friendship in an effort to free others from their addiction to violence.

We trust in God to act as we fulfill God's way of nonviolence; thus, we trust in the God who lives in every human being. We trust in the goodness and love in every human heart, even those who support injustice. Nonviolence encourages mutual trust. It upholds the truth of our spiritual unity as human beings and fosters reconciliation and friendship between enemies. To promote reconciliation, someone has to take the first step of trusting the other. Nonviolence invites us to take that step of unilateral trust in the other's basic goodness.

Nonviolence opens the door to a world where we can trust one another. As we grow in trust for one another, we will learn to trust God even more. In this process, God's reign of nonviolence comes to earth again.

The life of nonviolence is a daily effort to go deeper into the nonviolence of God. It does not wait for that moment when someone will do violence to us; it actively enters into the world's violence and seeks to transform it through God's nonviolent love. Nonviolence develops into a natural response of love and peace in all relationships.

Nonviolence invites us to pursue this spirit of love and reconciliation with our very lives. No matter how confusing or ineffective the way of nonviolence may appear, the vow of nonviolence commits us to that way and opens up the hope and vision of God's nonviolent reign. Such a commitment will be marked by joy and a deep reverence for all life.

In conclusion, the grace of God's nonviolence channeled through a vow of nonviolence will have consequences and implications in our lives if we are faithful to the vow. The vow of nonviolence commits us for life to God's way of nonviolence. Not only do we promise not to use violence and to transform the violence of the world, we seek to dwell in the nonviolence of God for eternity. Vowed nonviolence pledges not to waste life in the pursuit of money, honor, pride, power and violence, and thus death. The vow is a promise to die to self in pursuit of God's love and truth—and so to find life for ourselves and for suffering humanity. Faith, fearlessness, powerlessness, voluntary poverty, humility, mercy, and forgiveness— coupled with adamant nonviolent resistance to injustice— characterize this pledge of love and truth.

Through the vow of nonviolence, God is calling forth "a nonviolent army" to transform the earth into God's reign of justice and peace. As Gandhi dreamed, God seeks "soldiers of nonviolence"; practitioners of "militant nonviolence"; truth-seekers disciplined in thought, word, and deed to respond with and practice loving nonviolence in the struggle for justice and peace. Such love is painful and costly, yet ultimately victorious and Godlike.

By pledging the vow, a person prays, "Yes, I will try to practice nonviolence in the struggle for justice and peace and the search for truth even though I am sinful, weak, broken and usually not very helpful . . . but take me, God. Take my desire for justice and peace and do with me what you will. Disarm my heart and make me your instrument to disarm other hearts and the world. Transform my heart and my life and transform our world. In my life, continue your work of healing us all from our addiction to violence and lead us to the sober life of nonviolence."

The vow of nonviolence pledges that we will try to be saints, to love God, to accept the grace of God's nonviolence, to strive for holiness, to participate in the nonviolent coming of God's reign of justice and peace, and to witness to the gift of nonviolence which God offers us all. The vow commences a life of experimentation in truth. In the process of learning the truth, the vowed person will try to live truthfully, peacefully, no matter what the cost.

Through our vow of nonviolence, we will regularly ask God, "What do you want me to do right now for peace, for truth, for love, for justice, for those who are suffering from systemic violence, for the human family, at this moment and every moment in my life, especially in the light of your nonviolence?" The answer will take some form of active love that can help spark the nonviolent transformation of humanity.

7

The High Price of Nonviolent Love

ALL Christians are called to embrace nonviolence. Indeed, all human beings were created to live together in a spirit of nonviolence. Given this mandate of nonviolence, some people object to a vow of nonviolence. They suggest that a vow will limit the practice of nonviolence to the select few who profess it, forming a new elitism in the Christian community. Others claim that Christians cannot rightfully vow themselves only to one tradition in church teaching. Some argue that Jesus forbade the profession of vows when he commanded his followers not to swear at all. Finally, some dismiss nonviolence because they say it does not work. The answers to these and other questions can shed further light on our vow of nonviolence.

Nonviolence Is Normative

In discussions about the vow of nonviolence, people ask, "But are not all Christians called to be nonviolent?" If a select few profess themselves to nonviolence, it is argued, then others will begin to believe that nonviolence is just for the elite few who take a vow. There is no need to profess a vow of nonviolence, it is argued, because nonviolence is part of the very definition of our Christian discipleship. Every Christian is committed to Christ's nonviolence in their baptism.

A vow of nonviolence will simply promote the view that nonviolence is a charism or gift of the Spirit given to one group and not to every member of the body of Christ. As more people profess the vow, churches will begin to accept the error that not every Christian is called to nonviolence, only those who received the special grace of the vow. The vow of nonviolence then will encourage those who do not profess it to carry on with their violent ways.

I believe that active nonviolence is a moral imperative for every Christian. Nonviolence is normative for Christian life. Following Jesus in today's world means allowing God to disarm our hearts so we can become instruments for God's disarmament of the world. Following the nonviolent Jesus means becoming a people of nonviolence. It calls for active, public, creative nonviolence by every one of us.

Today most Christians continue to practice violence and believe that the mass murder of warfare and systemic violence is justified, even blessed by God. Christian churches have a long and sinful history of blessing and condoning violence—indeed of waging war and killing people. The renewed commitment of vowed nonviolence may help reverse that trend.

Historical research has revealed that for the first three centuries, the Christian community was pacifist. No Christian author at that time wrote of the Christian's duty to participate in war or in the military forces of the empire. To be a Christian in the years following the martyrdom of Jesus was to risk one's own life in a similar nonviolent struggle for justice and to pledge obedience to God, not to the empire.

"From the end of the New Testament period to the decade 170-180," writes historian Roland Bainton, "there is no evidence whatever of Christians in the army. . . . From that time on the references to Christian soldiers increase."[1] From the days of Jesus until the formal imperial edict of Emperor Constantine legalizing Christianity, many Christian writers made explicit condemnations of military service and professed Gospel peacemaking as a way of life.

"The early Christians took Jesus at his word, and understood his inculcations of gentleness and non-resistance in their literal sense," observes C. John Cadoux.

> They closely identified their religion with peace; they strongly condemned war for the bloodshed which it involved; they appropriated to themselves the Old Testament prophecy which foretold the transformation of the weapons of war into the implements of agriculture; they declared that it was their policy to return good for evil and to conquer evil with good.[2]

The early Christians understood that to follow Jesus meant renouncing violence and warfare and taking up his way of nonviolent resistance to evil. The nonviolence of Jesus was imperative for them; they gave their lives witnessing to the way of nonviolence. They did not have the word "nonviolence," but they spoke of "meekness," "gentleness," and "overcoming evil with good."

These original followers of Jesus formed a community of nonviolence which acknowledged Jesus as the Christ and risked arrest by disobeying the emperor's "divine" claims. Thousands of early Christians were arrested, imprisoned, tried, tortured, and martyred, just like Jesus. And like Jesus, they went to their deaths in a spirit of forgiving love. Such powerful nonviolence bore great fruit; it helped bring down the Roman empire. By the time Emperor Constantine officially recognized Christianity as the religion of the empire in the early fourth century, the nonviolent tradition of the church began to pass into desert monasteries, where it was reserved for those "called to perfection." [3]

With the development of the just war tradition and the holy war tradition, radical nonviolence began to disappear as a public witness of the church. Soon, Christians waged full scale wars and began to profit from such violence. The image of Jesus as a practitioner of nonviolence disappeared. They worshiped a god of violence and so lost touch with the nonviolent God of Jesus.

The time has come to return to the way of nonviolence and Jesus' image of a nonviolent God. The depths of our violence, even in the Christian community, are so deep that it may take generations of focused evangelization and witness to explain to Christians that to be Christian is to practice nonviolence and make peace.

Churches need to return to the grace of nonviolence and witness to the world about another way of life, the nonviolent alternative. The churches are called to proclaim to the world God's nonviolent reign of justice and peace.

We are all called to help transform the world, but to do so, we need to begin with ourselves. Because of our entrenchment in the ways of violence, some of us may have to work harder and concentrate on the commitment to Christian nonviolence by professing a vow. With the vow of nonviolence, we are not initiating a new Gnosticism, a new branch of belief that claims to have all the answers and the only way to God. Nor are we forming a new elitist group. Rather, in the vow of nonviolence, some Christians are finding a way to enter into God's renewal of the church and the world. Through the vow, we allow God to disarm our hearts so we can join the process of God's transforming nonviolence.

A vow of nonviolence may be an instrument of God which allows the Spirit of peace to breathe new life into the world. If many people live the vowed life of Gospel peacemaking seriously, they could model for the Christian community a new understanding of what it means to be a Christian. They could lead the Christian church away from just wars and systemic violence toward the way of nonviolence.

By professing a vow, some Christians may find strength and renewed motivation to be more active and zealous in pursuit of God's nonviolent reign. They may be better centered in the nonviolence of God and thus better prepared to resist the violence of the world. Vowed nonviolence may give new life to the Christian community which has become entrenched in power and warfare. It may be a way for Christians to return to their calling as God's sons and daughters, peacemakers, followers of the nonviolent Jesus.

Christians vowed to the way of nonviolence can help other Christians return to the Spirit of nonviolent love, peacemaking, and divine obedience that guided the original apostles, disciples, and martyrs of nonviolence. The vow may free Christians to break loose from the shackles of apathy and societal pressure to support systemic violence. It may help Christians to incarnate the Word which teaches that the way to right wrongs is to take on suffering, not inflict it. It could help us enter more fully into God's process of accepting suffering without retaliation for the transformation of the world.

Vowed nonviolence may be a good step for the Christian community's pilgrimage into the nonviolent reign of God. It may help us to reset our sights on God and to be more faithful to God's nonviolent reign which we have obstructed for so long.

The vow may encourage us to continue the struggle for justice and peace. We need to encourage one another to take biblical steps that will help us become instruments of God's peace.

The vow may help those Christians working in especially violent areas or places of "abstracted" systemic violence who are trying to overcome violence with nonviolence but are finding the long commitment difficult, draining, and nearly impossible. It may deepen our spiritual and actual commitment to peace and justice and heal our burnt out, embittered or despairing hearts.

The vow of nonviolence is especially fitting when seen in the light of Christian tradition. The possibility of Christians vowing themselves to Gospel nonviolence and universal suffering love continues the holy tradition in church history of public religious vows and private devotional vows which were the cause of great renewal at times in the church's history. The commitment to evangelical poverty made by Francis and his followers in the thirteenth century, for example, breathed a whole new spirit and way of life into Christianity which had long been forgotten.

Similarly, vows of nonviolence may breathe new life into the church in this age of global violence. The vow can be professed by anyone who longs to be more faithful to the way of nonviolence and wants to contribute to the birth of a nonviolent, peacemaking church for the twenty-first century.

Nonviolence Insists That War Is Never Justified

Those who do not accept Christian nonviolence and do accept the just war theory raise another objection: Can Christians rightfully vow themselves to only one tradition in Christian ethical teaching? They argue that the church has defended war for centuries, that indeed war is justified. They maintain that the church's primary response to war has been the just war theory of Augustine and Aquinas. How is a vow of nonviolence consistent with church teaching on war, some ask.

We believe nonviolence is a way of life open to all. Even the just war theory assumes that violence is not the ideal way to settle conflict. However, given the realities of nuclear warfare and the world's addiction to violence, many Christians are beginning to see that there is no such thing as a just war. The just war theory is no longer applicable, if it ever was, because once we permit killing, we open the door to global destruction. The acceptance of deterrence as a national policy is no longer acceptable either, for it intends to kill on a massive level.

It has taken a century of global violence that has threatened the destruction of the human race for Christians to realize that we are not allowed to kill, wage war, or support systemic violence. Christians around the world are developing new understanding and awareness. We are beginning to know God as a God of nonviolence, to see that Jesus is actively nonviolent, to recall that the early Christians were people of nonviolence. We too can live out our faith more fully if we adopt the way of nonviolence. We are beginning to hear Jesus when he says, "Love your enemies, do not kill them."

Christians are beginning to understand the lie of violence. Many Christians are waking up to the good news that God does not bless warfare, approve nuclear weapons, or condone injustice. God abhors starvation, murder, and other forms of violence. God wants us to live together in peace and justice as sisters and brothers.

With this insight into the God of peace, we can reject the just war theory and move into the way of nonviolence. Indeed if every Christian would embrace the way of nonviolence, the world would come much closer to God's nonviolent reign of justice and peace. We can heed the advice of the late Bishop Carroll Dozier who said, "The just war theory should be filed in the same drawer that contains the flat earth theory."

Nonviolence Opposes Legalism

Some people object to the profession of any kind of vow, arguing that Jesus was against vows. They cite the fourth antithesis of Matthew's Sermon on the Mount.

> Again, you have heard that it was once said to those of ancient times, "You shall not swear falsely, but carry out the vows you have made to the Lord." But I say to you, do not swear at all, either by heaven, for it is the throne of God, or by the earth, for it is his footstool, or by Jerusalem, for it is the city of the great King. And do not swear by your head, for you cannot make one hair white or black. Let your word be "Yes, Yes" or "No, No": anything more than this comes from the evil one. Matt. 5:33-37

This text teaches us not to take oaths and not to swear. It fits in with all Jesus' teachings on nonviolent resistance, for it tells us that when we are brought before the imperial courts which defend injustice and threaten us with violence, we are not to take an oath or to swear to tell the truth. Instead we are to remain consistent with our lives of active nonviolence, steadfast truth-telling, and peaceful resistance to the systems of violence and their courts of law. Tell the truth as you always do, Jesus says. Say "Yes" when you mean yes and "No" when you mean no. Such honesty is at the heart of nonviolence.

Jesus also commands us to avoid legalism, to not lose the Spirit of God, and to speak only the truth if we wish to follow him. This passage warns us that life in God is not to be lived in coercion or fear of punishment, but in the free spirit of truth. Too often, Jesus recognizes, we give into the fear of law and swear or make oaths that are to be obeyed under penalty of pain or death. Jesus opposes anything rooted in violence, including the law.

He would strenuously object to a coercive understanding of vows, whereby vows were to be enforced and mistakes punished just like the oaths of law. In an oath, God is called upon to witness to a truth, and thus to enforce through coercion any error or straying from that promise. In reality, if that oath is broken, it is not God who punishes us but the empire and governments which make violence legal and use violence to justify themselves.

Vows are different. Vows are professed to God and one another, not in a court, but in communities of nonviolent love as expressions of our deepest desires. Jesus teaches that we should not invoke God for our own purposes and expect God to punish us or punish each other in the name of God. Vows are public recognitions of what God has already done and the pledge of acceptance of and cooperation with this grace of God. They are not efforts to control God.

Christians have been making promises since the days of Christ in their baptisms and in their baptismal renewals. These promises express the longing of the catechumen and the Christian to be a new person in Christ, to continue to receive and live out the new life to which God has called them.

A sweeping rejection of all solemn promises and vows to God mistakes the proper understanding of a vow, confuses a vow with an oath, and runs in sharp contrast to one of the most ancient biblical practices. Vows are not oaths or pledges to a narrow-minded, limiting ideology. Vows are channels of God's grace and can help us become more human. They can help us fulfill God's law of love.

In light of Jesus' words, the vow of nonviolence is indeed a "Yes" to what God is doing in our lives. It is the public acceptance of God's gift of nonviolence. It says

"Yes" with all our hearts to God's way of life and promises to keep on saying "Yes" to God. In a vow of nonviolence, we say "Yes" to Jesus and his call to nonviolence. We promise to take our "Yes" seriously.

The "Yes" to God in vowed nonviolence is unlike any military oath or governmental oath. The vow is unlike the presidential oath taken under God's name to protect, defend, and uphold the Constitution of the warmaking United States. It is unlike Herod's oath to his daughter to give her whatever she wanted, including the head of John the Baptist.

The vow of nonviolence claims the search for truth through the flexible, discernible guidance of the Holy Spirit. The vow declares, "Yes, I will try to practice your way of nonviolence." It accepts the grace of nonviolence which God gives us; it does not need to swear anything. It is a response to an invitation from God, not a legalistic practice. It is lived out in freedom, not under coercion.

We know that Jesus said "Yes" to God's invitation to be nonviolent and was obedient to the nonviolence of God. To follow the nonviolent Jesus, we too are invited to say "Yes" to the God of nonviolence through this public vow.

Nonviolence Calls Us Beyond the Business of Religion

Some people maintain that Christians should not profess vows of nonviolence because the Pharisees of Jesus' day professed vows similar to what we call nonviolence. Jesus, these people say, was so opposed to the legalism and rigidity which the Pharisees practiced that he would oppose the vow of nonviolence.

The Pharisees were a Jewish party that refused to compromise their religious beliefs. Greatly respected by the people of Jesus' day, they followed a strict adherence to Hebrew law. Unlike the Sadducees, they were conservative in politics and generally rejected compromise with political rulers. As the Gospels make clear, Jesus had serious conflicts with the Pharisees (see Matt. 23:13-36). Such opposition reflects the early Christian communities' conflicts with the Pharisees; we need to remember the Gospels may give a more negative portrait than may always be fair to the Pharisees.

As best we can ascertain, however, the Pharisees were not pledged to what we would call active nonviolence. They were not pursuing the transformation of imperial violence through steadfast, nonviolent resistance. Some Pharisees, like most people of their day, practiced submission to the ruling authorities and the empire in the hope that a militaristic messiah would come. They wanted this warlike messiah to bring judgment, become their king, adopt the world's way of power and violence, and rule the earth. Such hopes trapped them and most others into silence and complicity in the face of imperial violence and oppression.

Indeed, though they may not have killed people themselves, they benefited from the systemic injustice of their day and condoned the killing of marginalized peoples. As with most people of their day, they supported systemic violence, injustice, and oppression. The "passivism" of the Pharisees was not the active "pacifism" of Jesus. They did not practice Jesus' revolutionary nonviolence. They were not scandalous; they were the epitome of mainstream religion.

The Pharisees profited from the status quo and so they never rocked the boat, like Jesus did. They did not practice the risky, dangerous nonviolence that insists on God's truth, opposes systemic violence, and threatens empires. Such passivity and complicity is not very different from the religious people of today who support the status quo's violence and injustice through their financial resources, their apathy, their complicity, and their justification of war.

The vow of nonviolence takes us beyond the institutionalized religion of the Pharisees into the martyrdom of Jesus and his followers who speak truth to power and resist the forces of violence and death. The vow promises that we will enter into the revolutionary nonviolence of Jesus. It pledges to follow Jesus as he continues to turn over the tables of the world's systemic violence. It is neither passive nor violent. It commits us to the disarming action of God which challenges us all.

Thus the vow threatens governments and empires because it promises to end systemic violence and transform everyone into people of nonviolence who will no longer support or condone violence. Indeed it transforms us into nonviolent resisters, willing to lay down our lives for our suffering sisters and brothers.

Nonviolence Works

Some people charge that a vow of nonviolence is a mistake because it does not work. Most people still do not understand what nonviolence is all about. Given the world's addiction to violence, most of us give in to despair and say there is nothing we can do to change the world. Most of us quickly forget Gandhi's nonviolent revolution in India, the nonviolent resistance of People Power in the Philippines, the nonviolent example of the Chinese students who stood up to tyranny. We forget the nonviolent civil rights movement of Dr. King which changed U.S. history, or the nonviolent demonstrations that brought down the Berlin Wall and the Soviet Union. Because nonviolence has rarely been tried, we presume it does not work.

This is not true. When active nonviolence has been used in history by large groups of people, it has always brought significant social change for justice and peace. The movements led by Gandhi and King accomplished sweeping reforms that changed the world, without much bloodshed compared to the violent movements of war which have taken the lives of hundreds of millions of people.

Most social change has been sought through violence. Most revolutions have involved killing people. Such violence only sows the seed for further violence. I believe (with Jesus and Gandhi) that there is nothing revolutionary about violent revolution. It adopts the same violent methods of the oppressors who have gone before us. It makes us into the very people we do not want to be. Under the guise of goodness, through the imperial logic of "any means necessary to get our end result," revolutionary violence leads only to a temporary victory. It does not break the cycle of violence but merely continues the world's addiction to violence and death.

Violence even in large-scale revolutionary movements never works because it only results in further death and division; it does not win over the opponent to the truth of justice and peace. It does not bring about the love and reconciliation which God's way of active nonviolence insures. It permits the violence of division to fester and ensures the outbreak of further violence somewhere down the line.

Because it is so costly, so daring, so scandalous, so open to God, large-scale, active, revolutionary nonviolence has rarely been tried. But when it has been tried with heartfelt conviction by many people, including ordinary people like us, it has worked miracles.

Because Gospel nonviolence is so rarely formally practiced in our world, because the world is so persuasive in telling us that violence is justified, many people still do not understand the power of active nonviolence. Active nonviolence always leads to further reconciliation, yet we may not see the results immediately. Because it uses peaceful means, nonviolence bears peaceful fruit.

Most important, however, nonviolence works because it is the way God has revealed to us. This is the method of social change that God has given us. God does not want us to kill people to change the world so that people will no longer kill people. Instead, God asks us to risk our lives in a nonviolent struggle for justice and peace. God asks us to stop the killing even in our revolutionary work for peace and justice. God promises to bless such nonviolent struggles with the fruit of God's nonviolent justice and peace. As we participate in God's nonviolent struggle, we participate in the coming of God's nonviolent reign.

Such nonviolence takes the long-haul view of history. It takes into consideration the spiritual consequences of violence and nonviolence and understands that God's way is a way of nonviolence. If we want to be faithful to God, if we want God's reign of real justice and peace to be present, we need to practice God's way of nonviolence.

Even if the way of nonviolence appears to fail, we are called to be faithful to this way of revolutionary change because it is of God. In such holy, revolutionary nonviolence, we need not be concerned with effectiveness or the possibility of getting killed. Though we strive with all our hearts and lives to end injustice, we do so because God asks us to do so and leave the outcome to God. We follow the lead of God, the example of Jesus, and trust that God will bring about God's reign. Nonviolence understands that the reconciliation we seek has already been won, that peace has already been given to us, that justice is already at hand, if we accept it.

If we are faithful to the way of nonviolence, we will appear to fail. Given the standards the world, where success is measured in the power to dominate and control others, the way of nonviolence can hardly be understood. But nonviolence does not play according to the rules of the world and its violence. It follows God's law of love. As

Jesus demonstrated, when the way of nonviolence is wholeheartedly pursued, it can quickly lead to crucifixion and martyrdom. We may appear to fail as Jesus "failed" when he was arrested and crucified.

But we know that accepting violence in the struggle for justice and even getting killed is not the end of the story. We know that God is not inactive, but raises those who pursue the way of nonviolence. We know that through our obedience to God's active nonviolence, God may use us to transform our world and raise us to everlasting life just as the nonviolent Jesus, executed as a revolutionary, was raised up.

When we declare that nonviolence does not work, we fail to see that God is a God of nonviolence and that God's nonviolence is the only thing that has kept us from destroying ourselves and the entire planet already. Without the spirit of nonviolence actively at work in the world for centuries, indeed without the nonviolence of Jesus, we would have long ago destroyed the earth. Nonviolence has already worked and is working in our hearts right now, taking us deeper and deeper into God's own peace. God's spirit of nonviolence is saving us all.

Nonviolence Finds Meaning in Suffering and Death

Many of us are confused by the idea of being willing to suffer without inflicting suffering on others as we struggle for justice and peace. The way of nonviolence invites us to take on the violence of the world as Jesus did. This is so that the violence will end (perhaps literally in our bodies) and we can all be transformed into a people and a world of nonviolence.

But nonviolence does not masochistically seek violence; we do not want to injure ourselves. We do not want to suffer violence; we want all violence to end. We want to transform violence through our nonviolence. We seek to overcome the violence in ourselves and others so that we may all be further reconciled and transformed. When we take such steps into the world of violence, and refuse to retaliate with further violence, it may appear to some that we are supporting violence, even encouraging it. In reality, we are uncovering the violence that is present everywhere, even within us, and breaking its never-ending spiral by not retaliating with violence. We break the cycle of violence every time we respond with nonviolent love.

Active love willing to suffer for justice's sake will provoke people to unleash the violence in their hearts. When they see that such violent action does not evoke violence from us, they will be disarmed and the cycle of violence will be broken. In this process, we can heal each other from our addiction to violence.

The liberation campaigns of Gandhi and King touched a nerve that unleashed the violence in their opponents and in society. These campaigns of nonviolence resulted in the temporary arrest and persecution of many people, and even in the death of some dedicated peacemakers— including Gandhi and King themselves. But the nonviolent love of Gandhi, King and their co-workers bore tremendous fruit. More people need to take up where these peacemakers left off in the nonviolent struggle.

The provocative love of Jesus, it has been said, caused people to do evil by crucifying him. But we know that the world of Jesus two thousand years ago was also addicted to violence and injustice. He confronted that world with his active nonviolence and his death led to his resurrection in his followers. Their ongoing campaign of nonviolent love transformed the Roman empire and led to the greatest movement in history, the movement of Christianity itself.

Jesus tried to tell us that we can do better than give in

to hatred and violence. Jesus showed us that the greatest thing we can do is to lay down our lives in the service of our suffering sisters and brothers. He invited us to become saints and martyrs. His resurrection showed us that death does not have the last word. We are all going to die anyway; Jesus asks us to offer a vision of nonviolence with our lives instead of continuing the downward spiral of violence.

Suffering and dying for the truth of God's nonviolence in the struggle for justice and peace are the most beautiful, fulfilling things we can do with our lives. The nonviolent, crucified Jesus who lives on in the struggle for justice says, "Do not be afraid. Trust in God and follow me along the way of nonviolence. Then your life, like mine, will bear the fruit of justice and peace for all." If we take Jesus seriously, we will not only help proclaim his reign of justice and peace, we will share in it forever.

Nonviolence Accepts Responsibility

It has been charged that nonviolence shirks the responsibility of defending ourselves and others from evil. If we were really committed, it is argued, we would use violence to defend ourselves and others.

The violence we use against each other violates the responsibility God gives us to care for and love one another. Nonviolence accepts full responsibility for the world's violence. It does not sit by and wait for the threat of violence. It enters into the fray of the world's violence right now.

Some objections to nonviolence reveal a deeper problem. Perhaps in our addiction to violence we are so filled with despair that we do not really want the peace and reconciliation God offers to us because it is so costly. Our fear and insecurity prevent us from trying this nonviolent alternative. We need to take a step along the way of nonviolence and see what happens. With each step, God's reign of justice and peace is proclaimed. Our challenge is to *try* nonviolence. This leap of faith will free us from our fears and insecurities, so we can accept responsibility and participate in the transformation of the world.

The way of nonviolence asks much of us. But nonviolence is worth the price, God insists. Nonviolence in practice is consoling, fulfilling, and joyful. It is a gift from God that is ours for the asking. Since God is so good and gives us the good gifts we ask for, often in better ways than we expected, we can be sure this grace will be given to us if we prayerfully ask for it and embark on God's way of nonviolence.

We cannot live nonviolence perfectly because we are sinful human beings and tend to forget who we are and what we are to do. We are all addicted to violence. But the God of nonviolence loves each one of us and is eager to help us become a people of nonviolence. God has led many people to live the way of nonviolence and many have been faithful to God's way of nonviolence. Any one of us can become a nonviolent person. All that is needed is the desire to live that life, the grace to accept God's disarming love, and the steadfast commitment to the nonviolent struggle for justice.

Because we admit that we can never be perfectly nonviolent, we surrender ourselves to the God of nonviolence in the hope that God will transform us and use us to transform our world. In this way, the Spirit of nonviolence and love will live and work through us. Nothing less than our very hearts and lives are required for this life of nonviolence. Yet this high price is small in comparison to the love, peace, justice, and reconciliation we will experience.

8

Gandhi and the Vow of Nonviolence

MOHANDAS Gandhi, the great apostle of nonviolence who coined the term *nonviolence*, was the first person to profess a vow of nonviolence. Perhaps more than any one else in an era of global violence, Gandhi revealed the potential of active nonviolence. For Gandhi, nonviolence was a way to transform the world's addiction to violence and injustice into a sober world of peace and justice. He dedicated his life to the pursuit of nonviolence. For him, taking a vow of nonviolence was essential. It bore tremendous fruit in his life and opened up the possibility of nonviolence for many others. Indeed, Gandhi showed us how the nonviolence of Jesus could be put into practice by millions to bring down an empire and possibly transform the world.

In his essay, "Pilgrimage to Nonviolence," Martin Luther King, Jr., paid tribute to Gandhi, acknowledging that Gandhi demonstrated to the world the nonviolence of Jesus.

> Gandhi was probably the first person in history to lift the love ethic of Jesus above mere interaction between individuals to a powerful and effective social force on a large scale. For Gandhi love was a potent instrument for social and collective transformation. It was in this Gandhian emphasis on love and nonviolence that I discovered the method for social reform that I had been seeking for so many months. . . . I came to feel that this was the only morally and practically sound method open to oppressed people in their struggle for freedom.[1]

"If humanity is to progress, Gandhi is inescapable," King wrote later. "Gandhi lived, thought, and acted inspired by the vision of humanity evolving toward a world of peace and harmony. We may ignore him at our own risk."[2]

The Nonviolence of Gandhi

"Nonviolence is the greatest and most active force in the world," Gandhi insisted. "One person who can express nonviolence in life exercises a force superior to all the forces of brutality."[3] "When the practice of nonviolence becomes universal, God will reign on earth as God does in heaven," Gandhi repeated throughout his life.[4]

"Nonviolence is the supreme law," he maintained. "During my half a century of experience, I have not yet come across a situation when I had to say that I was helpless, that I had no remedy in terms of nonviolence."[5] "Humanity can get out of violence only through nonviolence," Gandhi taught. "Hatred can be overcome only by love. Counter-hatred only increases the surface as well as the depth of hatred."[6]

After the United States dropped the atomic bomb on Hiroshima, Gandhi recognized that our need to commit ourselves to the way of nonviolence was more urgent than ever. "Unless now the world adopts nonviolence, it will spell certain suicide for humanity. . . . Nonviolence is the

only thing the bomb cannot destroy." [7] As King would declare two decades later, the choice for Gandhi was a choice
of nonviolence or nonexistence. Gandhi wrote,

> So far as I can see, the atomic bomb has deadened the finest
> feeling that has sustained humanity for ages. There used to
> be so-called laws of war which made it intolerable. Now we
> know the naked truth. War knows no law except that of
> might. The atom bomb brought an empty victory to the al-
> lied arms, but it resulted for the time being in destroying the
> soul of Japan. What has happened to the soul of the destroy-
> ing nation is yet too early to see. [8]

Gandhi hoped and prayed that humanity would rededi-
cate itself to the way of nonviolence. Today the world's addiction to violence still urges us to commit ourselves to
that way of nonviolence. "I have nothing new to teach the
world," Gandhi reiterated.

> Truth and nonviolence are as old as the hills. All I have
> done is to try experiments in both on as vast a scale as I
> could. In doing so, I have sometimes erred and learnt by my
> errors. Life and its problems have thus become to me so
> many experiments in the practice of truth and nonviolence. [9]

A Nonviolence of the Heart

Gandhi's nonviolence flowed from a disarmed heart.
"Nonviolence is a matter of the heart," Gandhi affirmed. [10]
"It is not a garment to be put on and off at will. Its seat is in
the heart and it must be an inseparable part of our very being." [11] He continued,

> Nonviolence that merely offers civil resistance to the au-
> thorities and goes no further scarcely deserves the name
> nonviolence. You may, if you like, call it unarmed
> resistance. . . . To quell riots nonviolently [for example]
> there must be true nonviolence in one's heart, a nonvio-

lence that takes even the erring hooligan in its warm embrace. Such an attitude . . . can only come as a prolonged and patient effort.[12]

Gandhi spent his life opening his heart to God so that God would disarm his heart and work for the disarmament of India and the world through him. His active, public nonviolence poured out from the nonviolence in his heart.

"Nonviolence cannot be preached," Gandhi maintained. "It has to be practiced." [13] Gandhi practiced nonviolence everywhere, with everyone, beginning with himself and extending to British royalty. This practice of nonviolence bore fruit, not only for the millions of people of India, but for the entire world. Gandhi asserted, "I have not the shadow of a doubt that any man or woman can achieve what I have, if he or she would make the same effort and cultivate the same hope and faith." [14]

Gandhi became a world leader who demonstrated how nonviolence could be *lived*—in the personal world of day-to-day life and on the public stage of international politics and revolution. His nonviolence became a threat to systemic injustice and imperial domination. Gandhi's nonviolence sparked nonviolent resistance in South Africa and nonviolent revolution in India. Perhaps even more importantly, it touched the spirit of humanity and inspired people around the world to seek peace with all their lives. Such explosive nonviolence, Gandhi learned, demands first and foremost a deep and thorough nonviolence of the heart.

Gandhi's Vow of Nonviolence

It is significant that Mohandas Gandhi saw the need in his life to profess a lifetime vow of nonviolence. His vow became a foundation for faith and trust in God from which he could risk his life for justice and peace. Gandhi struggled to be truthful and loving all his life. His determination to serve suffering humanity and to resist systemic injustice led him to God. Gandhi's whole life became a search for God through service to the poor and the nonviolent struggle for justice and peace.

As theologian Jim Douglass writes, Gandhi made God his end, "not as a terminal point and his particular salvation but as the Reality to be progressively found through his daily politics, the ground and measure of every decision and as an end already visible in the faces of people resisting oppression with love." [15] In this search for God, God revealed anew the way of nonviolence that Jesus had taught long ago.

While he was practicing law and serving the Indian community in South Africa, Gandhi's search for God led him (in 1906) to embrace celibacy. When he vowed—with the permission of his wife, Kasturbai—to be celibate, Gandhi discovered the grace "to live on the edge of a sword."

In his autobiography he noted,

> I realized that a vow, far from closing the door to real freedom, opened it. Up to this time I had not met with success because the will had been lacking, because I had had no faith in myself, no faith in the grace of God, and my mind had been tossed on the boisterous sea of doubt.[16]

The vow proved to be an instrument of strength, a channel of grace that drew him closer to God. This vow led him to promise lifelong nonviolence as well.

In September 1906, a bill was proposed by the racist South African legislature to require all Indians to carry registration cards. This law, like many other violations of civil rights, mobilized people anew to demand justice. Gandhi organized a mass meeting of Indians in Johannesburg to protest the bill. At that meeting he urged Indians to vow themselves to resist injustice through the steadfast commitment of nonviolence. "The government has taken leave of all sense of decency," Gandhi declared. "There is only one course open—to die rather than submit."

The struggle for justice would be long and demanding, Gandhi pointed out. "It will require that we risk arrest, imprisonment, starvation, torture, even death," he explained. "But I boldly declare, and with certainty, that so long as there is even a handful of people true to their pledge there can be only one end to the struggle—and that is victory."

Gandhi invited everyone present to join him in a pledge of nonviolent resistance to injustice and oppression, even unto death. They vowed to lay down their lives in this struggle for justice, but they promised they would never hurt or kill anyone. The audience stood, raised their hands, and vowed with Gandhi, "with God as our witness," not to submit to the ordinance if it became law.[17]

Through this experience, Gandhi learned that people had the strength to stand up to systemic injustice in a spirit of love, dignity, and truth. The vow of nonviolence unleashed a force of love and truth, and gave them new courage to resist injustice, even in the face of physical violence and death.

Back in India in 1919, when Gandhi entered the struggle for Indian independence, he urged his followers to vow nonviolence, to commit themselves to resist British oppression and systemic violence, but to do so in a spirit of love and truth that could transform India. In Bombay, Gandhi commented on these vows of nonviolence.

> Even such a mighty government as the government of Britain must yield if we are true to our pledge. For the pledge is no small thing. It means a change of heart. It is an attempt to introduce the religious spirit into politics. We may no longer believe in the doctrine of "tit for tat"; we may not meet hatred with hatred, violence with violence, evil with evil;

but we have to make a continuous and persistent effort to return good for evil. . . . Nothing is impossible. [18]

To be faithful to God's way of love and truth, Gandhi professed many vows and encouraged his community members in the Satyagraha Ashram at Sabarmati to join him. Together they pledged vows of truth, nonviolence, celibacy, fearlessness, control of the palate, non-possession, non-stealing, bread-labor, equality of religions, anti-untouchability, and *swadeshi* (using goods made only locally or within their own country). [19]

Gandhi later wrote about his vows,

Taking vows is not a sign of weakness, but of strength. To do at any cost something that one ought to do constitutes a vow. It becomes a bulwark of strength. . . . God is the very image of the vow. God would cease to be God if God swerved from God's own laws even by a hair's breadth. The sun is a greater keeper of observances; hence the possibility of measuring time and publishing almanacs. All business depends upon men and women fulfilling their promises. Are such promises less necessary in character building or self-realization? We should therefore never doubt the necessity of vows for the purpose of self-purification and self-realization. [20]

Gandhi adhered strictly to his vows of nonviolence and truth for the rest of his life. He stood up to violence, even the imperial violence of the British government. He met all people, including his British opponents, with a heartfelt love that transformed his opponents.

Gandhi's Commitment to Nonviolence

As Gandhi grew older and his experiments with nonviolence deepened, he discovered more possibilities for nonviolence. Gandhi became convinced that all persons could unleash the power of nonviolence by experimenting in their personal and public lives with the love and truth of God.

"My optimism," Gandhi explained, "rests on my belief in the infinite possibilities of the individual to develop nonviolence. The more you develop it in your own being, the more infectious it becomes till it overwhelms your surroundings and by and by might oversweep the world." [21]

The requirement for such deep, active nonviolence is a wholehearted, lifelong commitment to nonviolence. Gandhi wanted us to dedicate our hearts and lives to God's nonviolence, to spend our entire lives in personal and public pursuit of nonviolence so our hearts and world would be transformed into God's reign of nonviolence.

Nonviolence has to encompass every aspect of our lives so we come close to living in the very spirit of God's nonviolence. "Nonviolence to be a creed has to be all-pervasive. I cannot be nonviolent about one activity of mine and violent about others. That would be a policy, not a life force." [22] For Gandhi, nonviolence was not just a tactic, a strategy, a technique or a national policy; it was a life force and all-encompassing way of life.

"There is no such thing as defeat in nonviolence," Gandhi insisted.[23] "In nonviolence the masses have a weapon which enables a child, a woman, or even a decrepit old man to resist the mightiest government successfully. If your spirit is strong, mere lack of physical strength ceases to be a handicap." [24]

Gandhi hoped that one day communities, cities, and even nations of people would adopt nonviolence and so transform of the world. He wanted nonviolent governments and entire societies structured nonviolently, with nonviolent institutions that served the poor and brought justice. "We have to make truth and nonviolence not matters for mere individual practice but for practice by groups, communities, and nations. That at any rate is my dream. I shall live and die in trying to realize it." [25]

To this end, Gandhi believed that nonviolence had to be played out in the messy realities of the world's violence. To be faithful to the vow of nonviolence, Gandhi and his friends entered the struggle for justice and peace with all their lives and gave their lives to it.

> Nonviolence is not a cloistered virtue to be practiced by the individual for his or her peace and final salvation, but it is a rule of conduct for society. . . . I hold it therefore to be wrong to limit the use of nonviolence to cave dwellers (hermits) and for acquiring merit for a favored position in the other world. All virtue ceases to have use if it serves no purpose in every walk of life. [26]

During his life, Gandhi was beaten, thrown off a train, and threatened with death on many occasions, yet he clung to the spirit of nonviolence throughout these incidents. In the end, his very presence, so deeply rooted in nonviolence, sparked revolutionary, transforming change in people. As Daniel Berrigan once wrote, Gandhi was disarmed and dangerous. His disarmed heart was a dangerous threat to the empire and its violence.

Still Gandhi insisted on reconciliation, forgiveness, love, openness, and justice. His nonviolent witness inspired thousands of men and woman to join him in campaigns of nonviolence, even civil disobedience. The history of his life is marked with daily prayer, long fasts, years in prison, speaking out, writing, simple living, attempts to reconcile people, work on behalf of the poor, service to those in need, and solidarity with the poorest of the poor. He also carried out many campaigns for justice, such as the famous salt march of 1930.

Gandhi's life was a prayerful attempt to listen to the voice of God speaking to him, leading him, pointing him

in the right direction for justice and peace. This cooperation with God's grace brought him great peace of heart
and helped bring about the peaceful spirit he sought in
each campaign of nonviolence. It was precisely this powerful spirit of nonviolence that so attracted people to his
cause and so threatened the empire and its violence.

Gandhi's vow of nonviolence encouraged him to pursue the nonviolent love of God in the public arena, but it
also checked his pride and kept him humble. Remembering the violence of his early years and knowing how far
he still had to go, Gandhi placed his life in God's hands.
He knew that all his work for justice and peace was God's
work. He realized that he was still violent and untruthful
and constantly in need of God's disarming love.

Gandhi turned daily to the God of nonviolence
throughout his life. Every morning he prayed for a spirit of
nonviolence and promised God that he would be faithful
to his vow of nonviolence, saying,

> I will fear no one on earth today. I will fear only God. I will
> bear ill will to no one. I will accept injustice from no one. I
> will meet untruth with truth. In making truth known, I will
> accept all suffering.

Seven years before he was assassinated, Gandhi wrote,

> I have been practicing with scientific precision nonviolence
> and its possibilities for an unbroken period of over fifty
> years. I have applied it in every walk of life—domestic, insti-
> tutional, economic, and political. I know of no single case in
> which it has failed. Where it has seemed sometimes to have
> failed, I have ascribed it to my imperfections. I claim no per-
> fection for myself. But I do claim to be a passionate seeker
> after Truth, which is but another name for God. In the
> course of that search, the discovery of nonviolence came to
> me. Its spread is my life mission. I have no interest in living
> except for the prosecution of that mission.[27]

Gandhi's commitment to nonviolence pushed him to cross all barriers so that he could love his oppressors completely. He was always willing to forgive and compromise in the struggle for justice, knowing that his commitment to nonviolence, to the way of God, would eventually win. The effect of such disciplined, nonviolent love transformed all those he encountered, including the South African and British officials who opposed him. Gandhi wrote,

> It is no nonviolence if we merely love those that love us. It is nonviolence only when we love those that hate us. I know how difficult it is to follow this grand law of love. But are not all great and good things difficult to do? Love of the hater is the most difficult of all. But by the grace of God, even this most difficult thing becomes easy to accomplish if we want to do it.[28]

In this disciplined spirit of nonviolent love, Gandhi boldly declared toward the end of his life that he had ceased to hate people.

> I hold myself to be incapable of hating any being on earth. By a long course of prayerful discipline, I have ceased for over forty years to hate anybody. I know this is a big claim. Nevertheless, I make it in all humility. . . . But I can and do hate evil wherever it exists. . . . My noncooperation with evil has its roots not in hatred, but in love.[29]

The Art of Dying

The culmination of lifelong nonviolence is a death approached in a spirit of nonviolent love and peace. "Just as one must learn the art of killing in the training for violence," Gandhi observed, "so one must learn the art of dying in the training for nonviolence."[30]

Nonviolence is one of the world's great principles which no force on earth can wipe out. Thousands like myself may die in trying to vindicate the ideal, but nonviolence will never die. And the gospel of nonviolence can be spread only through believers dying for the cause.[31]

Gandhi's insistence on the art of dying well and the refusal to kill others demonstrates the revolutionary commitment of his nonviolence. Gandhi always said that our nonviolence is finally revealed to the world if we can die in a spirit of forgiveness and unconditional love while continuing to insist on truth and justice. In the summer of 1947, Gandhi said in a speech,

Have I that nonviolence of the brave in me? My death alone will show that. If someone killed me and I died with prayer for the assassin on my lips, and God's remembrance and consciousness of God's living presence in the sanctuary of my heart, then alone would I be said to have had the nonviolence of the brave.[32]

On January 29, 1948, in Delhi, the day before he was assassinated, Gandhi said to an associate,

Note down this also, that if someone were to end my life by putting a bullet through me—as someone tried to do with a bomb the other day—and I met his bullet without a groan, and breathed my last taking God's name, then alone would I have made good my claim.[33]

This is precisely what happened. When Gandhi was shot, he was walking to his regular session of evening prayer. He was making a greeting of peace and prayer toward his assailant when the bullets hit him.

Gandhi had learned the art of dying well. His life of prayer and nonviolence prepared him to meet his assassin in a posture of prayer and peace. He had trained all his life to live every moment in the fullness of nonviolence so that when death came, he would be well prepared to meet the God of nonviolence. This final act reveals that Gandhi lived out a disarmed heart open with love toward everyone, even those who would kill him.

The Depths of Gandhi's Nonviolence

Since Gandhi's nonviolence began in his heart, he knew that he had to let go of all pride, power, and ambition. Gandhi's nonviolence developed from a deep humility, even at the height of his fame. "I must reduce myself to zero," he kept telling himself.

> So long as a person does not of his [or her] own free will put himself [or herself] last among his [or her] fellow creatures, there is no salvation for him [or her]. Nonviolence is the farthest limit of humility.[34] I am but a poor struggling soul yearning to be wholly good—wholly truthful and wholly nonviolent in thought, word and deed, but ever failing to reach the ideal which I know to be truth. It is a painful climb, but the pain of it is a positive pleasure to me. Each step upward makes me feel stronger and fit for the next.[35]

The day before he was assassinated, when the writer Vincent Sheean asked for advice about living the life of active nonviolence, Gandhi replied, "Have nothing to do with power."[36]

Gandhi never wavered from his search for God and steadfast devotion to nonviolence. Gandhi characterized his life as an effort to achieve "desirelessness"—nonattachment to everything but God's truth of nonviolence. He understood nonviolence as a life of "long training in self-denial and appreciation of the hidden forces within ourselves." He described a person approaching nonviolence and desirelessness as someone

who is jealous of none, who is a fount of mercy, who is without egotism, who is selfless, who treats alike cold and heat,
happiness and misery, who is ever forgiving, who is always
contented, whose resolutions are firm, who has dedicated
mind and soul to God, who causes no dread, who is not
afraid of others, who is free from exultation, sorrow, and
fear, who is pure, who is versed in action yet remains unaf-
fected by it, who renounces all fruit, good or bad, who treats
friend and foe alike, who is untouched by respect or disre-
spect, who is not puffed up by praise, who does not go under when people speak ill of him, who loves silence and solitude, who has a disciplined reason.[37]

Such selfless love and devotion to God is the sanctity we
are all called to live, the ideal of the vow of nonviolence,
Gandhi suggested. Like Jesus, Gandhi believed such a life
was possible.

As Thomas Merton noted, the vow of nonviolence
helped Gandhi delve deep into that inner transformation
of nonviolence from which sprang Gandhi's public life of
transforming nonviolence. But toward the end of his life,
Gandhi was convinced that he had failed in his leadership
of the nonviolent campaign for independence. He realized
only in the mid-1940s, as the violence between Hindus
and Muslims exploded into riots, that the millions of Indians who had joined him in the nonviolent movement for
independence had not joined him as well in the revolutionary journey of inner transformation.

Gandhi concluded that his comrades in the independence movement had not pursued the disarmament of
heart which was at the center of public, active nonviolence. Their life work for peace and justice did not flow
from a unity of nonviolence already experienced inside
one's heart and soul. Merton writes,

The whole Gandhian concept of nonviolent action and satyagraha [soul force] is incomprehensible if it is to be thought as a means of achieving unity rather than as the fruit of inner unity already achieved. Indeed, this is the explanation for Gandhi's apparent failure (which became evident to him at the end of his own life). He saw that his followers had not reached the inner unity that he had realized in himself, and that their satyagraha was to a great extent a pretense since they believed it to be a means to achieve unity and freedom, while he saw that it must necessarily be the fruit of inner freedom. The thing of all and the most important of all was inner unity, the overcoming and healing of inner division, the consequent spiritual and personal freedom, of which autonomy and liberty were consequences.[38]

Merton recognized that it was from the love within Gandhi's heart and soul that Gandhi was able to practice nonviolence in the face of systemic violence and participate in the transformation of India.

Gandhi teaches us to pursue within ourselves the same revolutionary nonviolence that we pursue in the world. As Merton observes, our work for outer, nonviolent transformation will be actualized only if it flows from the inner revolution of active nonviolence at work in our hearts. Our movement for justice and peace begins in our disarmed hearts. God is pushing us into the world of violence so we can be instruments of God's nonviolent transformation.

Merton also saw the connection between a disarmed heart and public disarmament and Gandhi's vows of nonviolence and truth. These vows, Merton concluded, are

> the necessary preamble to the awakening of a mature political consciousness. They must be seen for what they are: not simply ascetic or devotional indulgences that may possibly suit the fancy of a few religious pacifists and confused poets, but precepts fundamentally necessary if humanity is to recover its right mind.[39]

For Merton, Gandhi was "a model of integrity whom we cannot afford to ignore, and the one basic duty we all owe to the world of our time is to imitate him in 'disassociating ourselves from evil in total disregard of the consequences.' "[40]

Gandhi's life has much to teach us about allowing God to disarm our hearts so we can cooperate with God's disarmament of the world. We can take heart from Gandhi's struggle and experimentation with lifelong nonviolence. We can also take courage realizing that Gandhi did not know exactly what would happen once he risked the life of nonviolence, yet, he remained faithful to that way.

Though a devout Hindu, Gandhi learned nonviolence from Jesus. His reading of the Sermon on the Mount deeply affected him and inspired him to live the life of nonviolence. Throughout his life, he turned to Jesus' teachings on nonviolence for insight and example. Gandhi wrote,

> Jesus was the most active resister known perhaps to history. This was nonviolence par excellence. . . . Jesus, a person who was completely innocent, offered himself as a sacrifice for the good of others, including his enemies, and became the ransom of the world. It was a perfect act. . . . Jesus lived and died in vain if he did not teach us to regulate the whole of life by the eternal law of love.[41]

As Gandhi learned nonviolence from Jesus, we too need to learn not only from Gandhi but from Jesus. Those of us considering the vow of nonviolence need to turn to the life of Jesus of Nazareth, the model of nonviolence, who shows us how to go deeper into the nonviolence of God. Let us turn now to our model.

9

Jesus, the Model of Nonviolence

IMAGINE the scene. Jesus is preaching in a crowded synagogue on the Sabbath. Suddenly he notices, sitting way in the back, a man with a withered hand. Jesus stops. He calls out to the man, "Stand up! Come out here in the middle."

The poor man stands up and comes up front to the middle near Jesus where he can be seen by everyone. Looking around the room, Jesus asks, "Is it against the law on the Sabbath to do good or to do evil? To save life or to kill?"

No one answers.

Jesus then says to the man, "Stretch out your hand."

The man obeys. He is healed.

The religious authorities are shocked. Their worship service has been disrupted. A poor, marginalized person has been placed in the center of the sanctuary. Jesus has scandalized everyone by breaking Sabbath decorum and posing tough questions about doing good, saving life, doing evil, and killing.

These are not permissible topics for such a sacred place. The focus of worship is to be on God, not on suffering people, they believe. Jesus has ruined everything. He has disrupted the religious authorities' comfortable life amidst a world of systemic injustice. They are so outraged, so threatened, that they immediately discuss killing Jesus (Mark 3:1-6).

Jesus is the model of active nonviolence. In this story, as usual, he deliberately breaks the law and custom which permits systemic injustice and suffering to continue. Jesus is public and provocative. He is a scandal and a threat to everyone in authority, to everyone but the poor and oppressed who find liberation in his way of life.

On that Sabbath day, Jesus could not continue to preach about God's way of life without stopping to heal the withered hand. Perhaps he could have waited until the next day to heal the man.

But Jesus always acts publicly to raise the question of life or murder. He knows that his nonviolent action will uncover and provoke the violence in us. He knows his actions will get him into trouble. Still he insists on nonviolence and reconciliation.

Jesus is the biggest troublemaker in the history of the world. Jesus insists on breaking through our addiction to violence, challenging our denial, confronting us with the truth, healing us with his nonviolent love, and offering us a way out of the world's madness into the nonviolent reign of God. Jesus acts nonviolently to resist the forces of violence and death and to reveal God's way of nonviolence and life.

Jesus Incarnates Nonviolence

The Gospels testify to the active nonviolence of Jesus. He is, as Gandhi wrote, the fullest expression of nonviolence, the model of nonviolence, the way of nonviolence. For

Christians, Jesus incarnates the nonviolence of God.

Jesus was born into a world of violence and injustice that oppresses the poor. He grew up in poverty on the fringe of a brutal empire. The Palestine of his birth reeked with injustice. The reign of Herod and Roman imperialism was marked with brutal repression against the poor. Anyone who questioned systemic injustice was tortured and publicly executed.

After the death of Herod the Great in the year 4 B.C.E., the son of a guerrilla leader who had been executed by Herod led a revolt on the Roman military arsenal in the town of Sepphoris (five miles southeast of Nazareth). The Roman military forces put down the violent revolution, burned Sepphoris to the ground, and enslaved many of its inhabitants.[1] In a final outpouring of imperial violence, Roman soldiers crucified some two thousand men on the road leaving Sepphoris. They saw this as an example and deterrent to the Jews and to all who questioned imperial domination.[2] Herod Antipas rebuilt Sepphoris and made it the temporary capital of the region.

The young Jesus would certainly have known about these atrocities. He might have witnessed the massacre and known people who were executed. Perhaps his father, Joseph the carpenter, and other carpenters had been hired or ordered to rebuild the city. Some wonder whether Joseph might have been one of those executed. Needless to say, Jesus understood the world's addiction to violence and injustice. He saw systemic violence and death up close from his youth and knew what he was talking about when he proposed God's way of nonviolent love as the solution to humanity's problems.

From this awareness of oppressive, repressive, and systemic violence, Jesus proposed the possibility of nonviolence. Unlike Jewish leaders such as the Pharisees, who profited from the imperial status quo, or the Zealots, who provoked revolution through murder and revolutionary violence, Jesus actively resisted systemic violence and the violence within the human heart. Jesus constantly proposed nonviolent alternatives. Throughout his life he embraced the way of nonviolence. His nonviolence was not passive nor private; it was active and public. Jesus' nonviolence so threatened the ruling, imperial authorities that he was executed as a revolutionary, in the company of other revolutionaries, the Zealots.

As Gandhi demonstrated 1900 years later, Jesus established that steadfast commitment to nonviolence was not only possible but could change the world. Through nonviolence Jesus turned over the tables of systemic violence and called for the transformation of humanity. He placed the choice of violence or nonviolence—indeed, nonviolence or nonexistence—squarely before his contemporaries. He urged his friends and followers to adopt, as he did, nonviolence as a way of life.

His relentless nonviolent resistance, his compassion and forgiveness, and his active love for others reveal the face of God. The God of Jesus is a God of love, peace, and nonviolence. Jesus was so revolutionary that he even changed our image of God, turning us away from a god of violence and war to the God of nonviolence and peace. Jesus proclaimed a God of unconditional love who does not bless systemic violence but calls us to transform violence through active nonviolence.

A Sermon on Nonviolence

According to the Gospel of Mark, Jesus began his public life after praying and fasting in the desert for forty days. After he heard that John the Baptist, the prophet of justice and peace, had been arrested by the authorities, Jesus traveled through Galilee proclaiming to the oppressed the good news of God's reign of justice and peace. This reign of nonviolence is at hand in the world of systemic violence, Jesus declared (Mark 1:14).

Repent, believe the good news of peace, become nonviolent, resist injustice, love your enemies, and forgive everyone, Jesus taught. Quoting Isaiah and Daniel, prophets of justice and nonviolence, Jesus invited everyone to love God by loving their neighbor. His way of unconditional, nonretaliatory, and sacrificial love became the hallmark of his teaching.

From the Sermon on the Mount to his parables about the reign of God to the Last Supper and his own execution, Jesus urged his followers to join God's revolutionary overthrowing of violence through nonviolence.

Jesus' fullest teaching on nonviolence, the Sermon on the Mount, is a manifesto of nonviolence. It proposes a way out of the world's addiction to violence through the sober method of nonviolent resistance. Instead of hating others and supporting the system of violence, Jesus calls us to love unconditionally, to hunger and thirst for justice, to risk our lives for peace.

Jesus' way of love knows no barriers. He wants us to break away from deterrence and love even our enemies. In so doing, we become like the God who loves everyone, even God's enemies. Such teachings reveal a God of nonviolence. By becoming people of nonviolence, Jesus proclaimed, we become the very sons and daughters of God.

The sermon on nonviolence begins with the Beatitudes, which affirm all who practice the nonviolence of God. In this sermon, Jesus affirms the life of steadfast nonviolence. That life for Jesus includes poverty of spirit, mourning (mourning the deaths of nonviolent resisters and poor people killed by the empire); meekness (peaceful, active resistance to systemic injustice); pursuing justice; being merciful; living out of a disarmed heart; making peace; and a willingness to suffer and die without retaliating.

To the poor of Galilee, Jesus proclaimed,

> Blessed are the poor in spirit, for theirs is the kingdom of heaven.
> Blessed are those who mourn, for they will be comforted.
> Blessed are the meek, for they will inherit the earth.
> Blessed are those who hunger and thirst for righteousness, for they will be filled.
> Blessed are the merciful, for they will receive mercy.
> Blessed are the pure in heart, for they will see God.
> Blessed are the peacemakers, for they will be called the children of God.
> Blessed are those who are persecuted for righteousness' sake, for theirs is the kingdom of heaven.
> Blessed are you when people revile you and persecute you and utter all kinds of evil against you falsely on my account. Rejoice and be glad, for your reward is great in heaven, for in the same way they persecuted the prophets who were before you. (Matt. 5:3-11)

For Jesus, the reign of God belongs first and foremost to the poor and to those persecuted in the nonviolent struggle for justice. The Beatitudes point to a way of nonviolence which Jesus then addresses directly in six concrete steps. Not only are we not allowed to kill, he says, but we are not even to get angry with one another. We are to seek reconciliation with our sisters and brothers above all else.

Reconciliation with humanity takes priority even over worship of God, according to Jesus' revolutionary nonviolence (Matt. 5:23-24). When we have renounced violence, once we are reconciled with everyone, and are committed to God's way of nonviolence, then we can worship the God of peace in peace.

The active nonviolence of Jesus becomes specific when he invites us to a life of nonviolent resistance to evil. We are to resist violence by non-cooperating with violence. We are not to return violence with violence but are to insist on our shared humanity so that God's reign of justice can break through, as the following text explains:

> Do not resist an evildoer. But if anyone strikes you on the right cheek, turn the other also; and if anyone wants to sue you and take your coat, give your cloak as well; and if anyone forces you to go one mile, go also the second mile. Give to everyone who begs from you, and do not refuse anyone who wants to borrow from you. (Matt. 5:38-42)

Jesus' way of nonviolent resistance is a direct challenge to the Zealots and other violent revolutionaries of his age. He supported their passion for justice, but, as Gandhi explained, Jesus refused to kill or use violence in that struggle for justice.

Jesus was as committed to justice and peace as the most devout revolutionary. Indeed, he was more committed because he refused to use the violent methods of the imperial forces. Jesus' way of nonviolent resistance is the most radical form of revolution in history. By inviting people to turn the other cheek, Jesus was not encouraging passivity or apathy; he wanted people to stand up, to remain dignified and resist every form of humiliating violence—but without violence. He urged noncooperation with evil and transformation of violence through a steadfast love and truth willing to suffer and die for justice and peace.

In this text, Jesus gives three specific examples of nonviolent resistance. First, when he speaks of being struck on the right cheek, he is aware that when one person punches another, he usually uses his right hand to hit an opponent on the left cheek. Thus the specific reference to being struck on the right cheek refers to the back-handed strike of a dominating person over a slave.

Jesus addresses the violence that humiliates and oppresses people. His response is the noncooperation which turns the other cheek and thus breaks the humiliation. This response upholds dignity, breaks the cycle of oppressive violence, and leads to justice.[3]

Second, Jesus confronts the Roman policy which leaves the impoverished masses in hopeless debt. Only the poorest of the poor would have nothing but an outer garment to give for a loan.[4] But when Jesus urges his followers to give up their inner garments as well when told to pay their debts to the empire—and thus to stand completely naked before the imperial court—he invites nonviolent direct action that challenges systemic injustice and disarms everyone.

As Walter Wink writes, nakedness was a scandal, not just to those naked, but even more so to the devout Jews and authorities who were exposed to it. Jesus' suggestion would cause considerable scandal, expose the lawsuit of the oppressors, uncover the injustice, and lead to the repentance of the oppressor. His nonviolent action could lead to the transformation of society if adopted by the poor.[5]

Third, Jesus challenges the Roman soldiers who force the poor to carry the soldiers' packs. According to the law, the soldiers were not to force people to carry the packs for more than one mile. In practice, however, the poor felt the weight of imperial oppression.

Jesus turns the tables on Roman superiority and shows the poor how they can assert their dignity and uphold their humanity. Jesus is not urging revenge or telling people to retaliate with humiliation; rather, he offers a way to help oppressing soldiers see that the poor they are burdening are their fellow human beings. The creative response of carrying the pack farther may help the soldier recognize the humanity in the poor person and lead to conversion and an end to the oppression.[6]

Jesus' way of nonviolent resistance reaches a peak

when he invites people to the nonviolence that loves the enemies of one's country. Jesus calls for a love that transcends national borders, that reaches out like the love of God to every human being, particularly the victims of one's country and its wars.

> You have heard that it was said, "You shall love your neighbor and hate your enemy." But I say to you, Love your enemies and pray for those who persecute you, so that you may be children of your Father in heaven; for he makes his sun rise on the evil and the good, and sends rain on the righteous and the unrighteous. For if you love those who love you, what reward do you have? Do not even the tax collectors do the same? And if you greet only your brothers and sisters, what more are you doing than others? Do not even the Gentiles do the same? Be perfect, therefore, just as your heavenly Father is perfect. (Matt. 5:43-48)

When our love transcends borders, when it reaches out to those who suffer from our warring violence, when it breaks the laws of empire and nationalism in a loving civil disobedience—then our love, according to Jesus, resembles God, who loves everyone everywhere in the world. God does not see borderlines or fences. God only sees the love in our hearts, (as Mother Teresa writes). God's love is so nonviolent that it transcends into every human heart.

Jesus wants us to love similarly. He wants us to break the laws which tell us who to love and who not to love. He wants us to practice the nonviolence of God, which will bring down empires and transform the world. When fully practiced, such love will mark the nonviolent reign of God on earth. This is the meaning behind the exhortation to be "perfect" like God. We are called to the great love of active nonviolence which reaches out to everyone. This is the nature of Jesus' love, which crossed national and cultural borders, offended the ruling authorities who finally executed him, and continues to transform our world.

The command to love enemies not only rules out warfare; it is the ultimate solution to war. Jesus wants us to transform the world with an all-embracing love. If we love our enemies, we cannot kill them or threaten them. Jesus rules out war as a response to human division and conflict.

When we take this vision of Jesus' nonviolence seriously, wars will end and injustice will cease. The entire weapons industry will close, the Pentagon will become a shelter for the homeless, and all battleships and military aircraft will be rededicated to the distribution of food and medicine to the poor of the world. The reign of God's love will extend to everyone.

A Vision of Lifelong Nonviolence

Jesus offers many practical suggestions for the life of nonviolence. He recommends giving our possessions away, praying regularly in solitude, fasting, trusting wholeheartedly in God, and setting our hearts on God and God's reign of justice and peace.

Jesus calls for a simplicity of life and a radical dependence on God. He suggests that his followers become like trusting children. "Do not worry and do not judge others," he said. "Speak the truth, seek justice for the poor, resist systemic injustice, love unconditionally, make peace, forgive everyone, do not do violence to anyone, and be like God. Take up the cross of nonviolent resistance to systemic injustice, struggle for justice and peace, accept the consequences of your truth-telling and follow me." For Jesus, the way of nonviolence is simple and clear.

Jesus was not afraid. Throughout his life, he urged his disciples not to be afraid. He teaches us not to fear the powers of violence and death. He shows a way out of our fears by encouraging us to place our trust in God.

If we place all our trust in God, Jesus suggests, then we

will have no trust left to place in the systems of violence, their idols, or their rulers. When religious authorities try to trap Jesus by asking him, "Should we pay taxes to Caesar?" Jesus asks the questioners if they have a coin to show Jesus. (Coins would have been inscribed with words "Caesar, the Divine One." Jewish leaders were not to carry such coins.)

When presented with a coin, Jesus exposes the trust people place in money and empires, rather than God. "Give to Caesar what is Caesar's, but give to God what is God's," Jesus responds (Mark 12:13-17).

As Dorothy Day once explained, once we give everything to God that belongs to God, there is nothing left to give to Caesar, the Roman empire, the systems of violence; or to their modern-day counterparts—U.S. presidents, nuclear weapons, and the structures of injustice. The nonviolence of Jesus demands allegiance to God alone; not a penny goes to the empire and its system of death.

In the portrait of the last judgment (Matt. 25:31-46), Jesus teaches that God dwells in every human being and that all people are equal. Jesus says that whatever one does to another human being, one does to a sister or brother and thus to God. This parable completes the vision of the Sermon on the Mount by revealing that God takes sides with the poor and the oppressed of the world and invites us to do the same—to make a preferential option for the poor. If we do this, we shall be reconciling the world, ourselves, and all humanity to God.

On that day God will say to those who served the poor and the oppressed of the world,

> Come, you who are blessed by my Father, inherit the kingdom prepared for you from the foundation of the world; for I was hungry and you gave me food, I was thirsty and you gave me something to drink, I was a stranger and you wel-

comed me, I was naked and you gave me clothing, I was sick
and you took care of me, I was in prison and you visited me.
Truly I tell you, just as you did it to one of the least of these
who are members of my family, you did it to me. (Matt.
25:34-36, 40)

With this story, Jesus invites us to remember that we are
all one family, all equal. If we are true to the reality of human unity, we will treat one another as sisters and brothers, beginning with the poorest people in the world. When
our love is put into practice, we will be loving God who
dwells with all those who suffer oppression and injustice.

A Campaign of Nonviolence

While teaching his disciples the way of nonviolence, Jesus
practiced a public campaign of revolutionary nonviolence.
He began in the poverty-stricken outskirts of war-torn
Galilee and journeyed into mainstream religious, imperial,
and cultural life in Jerusalem itself.[7] Time after time, he
risked arrest by confronting the laws and authorities who
supported systemic injustice. His dramatic confrontation
of nonviolent direct action in the temple in Jerusalem cul-
minated a campaign of nonviolent confrontation.

Jesus was determined to speak out against systemic injustice and to proclaim God's reign of nonviolence and
justice. That was the number one priority in his life. With
his love and nonviolence, he wanted to transform his
world and everyone in it.

Jesus' provocative nonviolence is portrayed over and
over in the Gospels. Accounts include the time his disciples picked corn illegally on the Sabbath, his associations
and meals with marginalized peoples, his healing people
in public places, and his challenge of the laws which made
oppression the norm. "You would not believe the trouble
we had from this guy," we read between the lines of the
Gospels.

Jesus practiced nonviolent civil disobedience everywhere he went. He challenged the authorities who supported and blessed the institutionalized violence of his day. To the poor who followed him, he offered love, encouragement, and the positive alternative of nonviolent resistance. He called these friends to give their lives in the nonviolent struggle for justice. In this life of active nonviolence, they were to "love one another," he declared. Jesus' revolution was rooted in love. "A person can have no greater love than to lay down her life for her friends," he proclaimed.

Jesus was not passive. Instead he provoked trouble by exposing violence, promoting nonviolence, and calling for conversion. Having taught nonviolence and love of enemies, it was fitting for Jesus to put aside his own fears and to invite others to put aside their fears and live in the reign of God's peace.

He could have remained in Galilee and continued his "successful" ministry of preaching. He could have lived a life of respect and adulation. His friends urged him to avoid Jerusalem because they knew he would get into trouble.

By going to Jerusalem he engaged in nonviolent direct action in the face of systemic injustice and risked public execution on a cross. He showed through his actions and the ultimate action of laying down his life for others how to live out nonviolence. He showed that nonviolence includes speaking out the truth of God's reign of justice and peace, resisting the systemic injustice and imperial violence which oppress people, and loving everyone, even those who would kill us.

The decision to go to Jerusalem marked the depth of Jesus' commitment to nonviolence because he knew, as his disciples did, that his revolutionary appeal to nonviolence would probably cost his life. Nonetheless, he called on the authorities and all the people of Jerusalem to return to their roots as sons and daughters of the God of peace.

Jesus understood the political and social climate of his day. He knew that its systemic violence was leading toward destruction (as was realized in the year 70). Going to Jerusalem was an act of trust in God. It was a dangerous mission, but for Jesus, nonviolence demanded action and peaceful confrontation with the powers of violence in the hope of nonviolent transformation and new life.

When Jesus arrived at the temple, the center of the Jewish world, he found people buying and selling, oppressing the poor, ignoring the priorities of justice and peace, and not worshiping God. He committed an act of nonviolent civil disobedience by turning over the tables of the money changers and blocking the entrance to the temple (Mark 11:15-19; Matt. 21:12-13; Luke 19:45-46; John 2:14-16).

The temple exploited the poor masses by forcing them to pay a fortune for the opportunity of worshiping God. Jesus' nonviolent direct action called for an end to religious injustice, the business of making money off the poor in the name of a religion supporting the empire and its systemic injustice.[8] Jesus wanted the people to worship God in spirit and truth, to remember who they were and who they were called to be, a people of God's nonviolent love. He was willing to accept the consequences for speaking the truth. Upon this act of civil disobedience, the authorities immediately planned Jesus' death.

Jesus' civil disobedience in the temple was explicitly nonviolent. He did not hurt anyone. He did disrupt the business dealings and the comings and goings of the temple. Unfortunately, this provocative action has been used for centuries to justify violence, even nuclear war. People point to this dramatic episode and conclude that Jesus used violence, therefore we can kill people.

Such conclusions miss the point. Jesus did not kill anyone; he was nonviolent. His nonviolence was illegal and dramatic and specifically aimed at stopping wars and the systems that kept people oppressed and poor. This passage does not justify murder, injustice, or war. If anything, the story of this culmination of a life of nonviolent action should inspire millions of Christians to disrupt all places of war and institutionalized violence through peaceful, prayerful, nonviolent resistance. The account should challenge us to turn over the tables of systemic injustice and the imperial business of war that continues today.

Jesus' campaign of nonviolent resistance can be compared to nonviolent resistance by a Salvadoran campesino who confronts the U.S. embassy in San Salvador—the headquarters for the war that raged from the 1970s into the 1990s. A campesino from the northern province of Chalatenango, El Salvador, victim of U.S. bombing raids and systemic injustice, walks for days to San Salvador, the capital city. There he goes to the U.S. embassy, headquarters for the war and the status quo of injustice.

He enters the building and nonviolently turns over the tables in the offices, disrupting the work of the embassy. He sits down at the entrance and says that God does not want us to kill but to serve life. He commits a nonviolent, symbolic act of resistance. He does not hurt anyone or kill anyone, but he disrupts the normal routine of government, injustice, and warfare. His message is rejected. The campesino is immediately arrested, "disappeared," tried in an overnight court, and publicly executed.

Such was the nonviolence of Jesus. Similar nonviolent actions and disappearances occur regularly today throughout the world.

When Jesus was brought before the government leaders a few days after his action in the temple, he was charged with "perverting our nation, forbidding us to pay taxes to the emperor, and saying that he is the Messiah, a king" (see Luke 23:2). His accusers persisted, "He stirs up the people by teaching throughout all Judea, from Galilee where he began even to this place."

Jesus' way of active nonviolence threatened the religious and civil authorities because they knew if people adopted Jesus' way of nonviolence, the systems and structures of imperial violence and injustice would fall. The authorities realized that they would lose their power if enough people believed and acted on Jesus' nonviolence. If people obeyed God, loved one another, and resisted systemic injustice, as Jesus urged, the ruling authorities would lose the blind obedience of the masses. Their profits would cease and an entirely new society would develop.

The authorities realized people were listening to Jesus, that some were following him in his campaign of revolutionary nonviolence. They executed him to protect the empire's way of violence. But they did not understand the depth of God's nonviolence.

The Nonviolence of Jesus on the Cross

The night before he died, when he knew the authorities would soon arrest and kill him for his nonviolent action, Jesus brought his friends together. He encouraged them to form a community of nonviolence, to live together as God's children, to share a meal together in memory of him and his nonviolent way. He instructed his friends to serve one another as he did that night by symbolically and actually washing one another's dirty feet.

As the hour of his arrest approached, Jesus prayed in the garden of Gethsemane for strength to persevere in God's nonviolence. "God, let your will be done, not mine," he prayed. When the soldiers arrived, threatened to arrest everyone and asked for Jesus, he said, "If you are looking for me, let these others go." (John 18:8) He was arrested on charges of subverting the system and taken away as a criminal.

Jesus remained faithful to the way of nonviolence. He did not return the violence used against him because he knew that the people who were killing him were his brothers and sisters. They were children of God, and he wanted to transform them from their ways of violence. He wanted all the world's violence to end, right there and then, even in his own body if necessary.

When questioned by the high priest, Jesus answered, "I have spoken openly to the world; I have always taught in the synagogues and in the temple, where all the Jews come together. I have said nothing in secret. . . . Ask those who heard what I said to them. They know what I said" (John 18:20-21).

After Jesus said this, a guard slapped Jesus in the face and asked, "Is that how you answer the high priest?" (John 18:22)

Jesus spoke up. He did not strike back, but turned the other cheek and spoke the truth. "If I have spoken wrongly, testify to the wrong. But if I have spoken rightly, why do you strike me?" (John 18:23)

After Jesus was condemned to death by the authorities, he was punched, spat on, blindfolded, hit in the face with fists, and mocked. Jesus suffered the full force of the world's addiction to violence; he died under the full weight of imperial violence. He experienced terrible torture and agony, but throughout he remained centered in the spirit of God's nonviolent love. In his agony, he refused to resort to the violence used against him.

The peace and love Jesus manifested while undergoing such brutal torture and public execution reveal the profound depths of his nonviolence—indeed, the divinity of his spirit. Jesus incarnated nonviolence. He was a Messiah of nonviolence who broke the world's addiction to violence. He helped change history by opening up the possibility of steadfast, committed nonviolence.

When standing before Pilate, he declared, "My kingdom is not from this world. If my kingdom were from this world, my followers would be fighting to keep me from being handed over to the Jews. But as it is my kingdom is not from here. . . . For this I was born, and for this I came into the world, to testify to the truth. Everyone who belongs to the truth listens to my voice" (John 18:36-37). Under the reign of Jesus, violence is not used, allowed, or accepted. Violence is not an option.

Jesus was betrayed and denied by close friends, scourged, crowned with twisted thorns, and dressed in a purple robe. After carrying the cross, he was stripped and nailed to the cross, suffering physical agony and verbal abuse. In the torment of crucifixion, Jesus responded with pure nonviolence, continuing to see his persecutors as children of God. Instead of hating those who were executing him, he took the most courageous step possible—he forgave his executioners and all who had hurt him. He prayed for them, "God, forgive them. They do not know what they are doing."

Jesus recognized that his enemies had forgotten who they were and who they were called to be. He forgave them and continued to love them, revealing the power of God and the spirit of nonviolence dwelling in his heart. On the cross, Jesus was completely disarmed. Indeed, Jesus went to his death as he lived his life: completely unarmed. Even in death, he disarmed others by responding with love, forgiveness, and truth.

He was jeered at by passersby as he was dying, and yet he remained faithful to who he was and to the God of nonviolence. Though misunderstood, he trusted God, hoping in God's transforming love even when there was little cause for hope. Jesus' final words convey the life commitment of nonviolence: "God, into your hands I commend my spirit."

Jesus was a victim of the death penalty. He was legally executed by the system. Crucifixion was a form a capital punishment like the electric chair or the gas chamber. Jesus' death on a cross was a scandal to his family, friends, followers, and countrypeople. In dying so scandalously, Jesus had failed in the eyes of his followers. He was completely misunderstood. Though few if any had grasped his message of nonviolence, though he was alone and rejected except for a handful of faithful women, he hoped in God.

Jesus lived every moment of his life knowing that the God of nonviolence reigns and calls us to become a people of nonviolence. He gave up his life for the coming of God's reign of nonviolence. On the cross Jesus revealed and became the fullest expression of God's reign of nonviolence.

The crucified Jesus represents a new image of a God willing to die for justice and peace but not willingly to kill. The image of God revealed by Jesus on the cross is a God who calls people to nonviolence. The crucified nonviolent Jesus died inviting others to follow him on his way into the paradise of nonviolence. Because his death so fulfilled this nonviolent love, he redeems us and shows us a way out of our addiction to violence and death.

The Nonviolence Which Rises and Overcomes Death

The words spoken to the women who came to the tomb of Jesus that following Sunday morning proclaim the victory of nonviolence. "There is no reason to be afraid," an angel declared. "I know you are looking for Jesus who was crucified. He is not here, for he has risen. Return to Galilee and you will find him there."

These are challenging words of great joy and wonder.

The resurrection of Jesus is God's ultimate affirmation of the way of nonviolence. The resurrection proclaims that Jesus' vision of nonviolence was correct and that he was right to resist systemic violence through a spirit of steadfast nonviolence.

The resurrection of Jesus is evidence that his message and humble life of nonviolence are the right way to live. By raising Jesus, God invites all people to follow Jesus, the way of nonviolence, to resist death and risk eternal life and so participate in the nonviolent transformation of the world.

The angel's words gladden our hearts with the good news that Jesus is alive. They also terrify us because they invite us to start the life of Jesus all over again. They urge us to go back to Galilee, into the world of oppression and injustice, and take up Jesus' campaign of nonviolent resistance. The angel's words send us into modern-day Jerusalems and their Pentagons with acts of nonviolent civil disobedience for the sake of justice and peace.

The risen Jesus Christ transformed his disciples and changed their lives. Now they understood his way and saw he was right to go to Jerusalem, to turn over the tables of systemic injustice, to call people to God's nonviolent love. They saw that Jesus' crucifixion had been legal. They were shocked to find him continuing his civil disobedience by illegally rising from the dead.

As Daniel Berrigan writes, according to the laws of empire, dead people are supposed to stay dead. Jesus broke the laws of death. The disciples no longer misunderstood the folly of the cross, the scandalous love which resists injustice through active nonviolence. They began to speak out around the world about God's way of nonviolent resistance and active love.

Thereafter, the disciples practiced the nonviolent, suffering love of Jesus as the way of God. From then on, they practiced nonviolent resistance. Thousands were arrested, jailed, tortured, and executed for insisting on the nonviolent reign of God. Through the resurrection they understood that God is indeed reigning, that God actively resists institutionalized violence. They saw that the God of nonviolence is stronger than violence or death itself. They recognized that if we place all our trust in God and follow the way of nonviolence, everlasting life and nonviolent love will reign in our hearts.

The death and resurrection of Jesus as the culmination of his life of nonviolence, they concluded, had indeed transformed the world. They became nonviolent resisters and followed him in acts of nonviolent resistance that ended in their own martyrdom—and resurrection.

The first gift the risen Jesus gave his disciples was the Spirit of nonviolence. "Peace be with you," he said. In the resurrection of Jesus, the fullest demonstration of God's active nonviolence, we are offered God's gift of peace, "a peace which the world cannot give." We are offered the fruit of Jesus' suffering love, the peace of God's reign.

Jesus' gift of peace is an invitation to a world without war and injustice, an invitation to follow him along the way of nonviolence. After his resurrection, Jesus explained to his disciples that he had tried to witness to the way of nonviolence all his life.

> "These are my words that I spoke to you while I was still with you—that everything written about me in the law of Moses, the Prophets and the psalms must be fulfilled." Then he opened their minds to understand the scriptures, and he said to them, "Thus it is written, that the Messiah is to suffer and to rise from the dead and on the third day, and that repentance and forgiveness of sins is to be proclaimed in his name to all nations, beginning from Jerusalem. You are witnesses of these things." (Luke 24:44-49)

The resurrection of Jesus helped his disciples understand nonviolence. They were transformed and began to
live according to his nonviolence. The risen Jesus commissioned them to teach everyone about his life of nonviolence and the good news that everyone can live this new
way of life. Jesus sent his disciples out as ministers of reconciliation who would reunite the human family, work to
end violence, and create a community of love and peace.

The risen Jesus said to his friends, "Go, make disciples
of all nations. Baptize them . . . and teach them to observe
all the commands I gave you. And know that I am with you
always; yes, to the end of time." In this final invitation, Jesus reiterated what he had said in the Sermon on the
Mount. "Let your light shine before others, so that they
may see your good works and give glory to your Father in
heaven" (Matt. 5:16).

Jesus commissioned his friends to proclaim, practice,
and live the way of nonviolence that he had incarnated.
"Go and act nonviolently," he said. "Love one another.
Speak the truth. Seek justice for the poor. Resist the violence of the world. Help others to become peacemakers.
Practice my way of nonviolence even unto death. Together, we shall enter into God's reign of nonviolent love."

Jesus and the Vow of Nonviolence

The vow of nonviolence is a pledge to continue Jesus' way
of nonviolence. It accepts Jesus' mission to transform the
world into God's reign of nonviolence. The vow of nonviolence commits us to his lifelong mission of nonviolence.
It can help us be faithful to Jesus' life of active nonviolence.
It can be a channel for Jesus' spirit of nonviolence to work
in us, disarm our hearts, and participate in God's disarmament of the world.

The vow can empower us to continue being the body
of Christ in the world today—as we fast, pray, dialogue, ac-

company the poor, resist injustice, act nonviolently, risk our lives in the nonviolent struggle for justice and peace, and follow Jesus to the cross and resurrection. The vow can help us to become faithful followers of the trouble-making, nonviolent Jesus.

In a world that continues to reject nonviolence, a vow of nonviolence can inspire us to a single-minded life of active nonviolence. Then God's reign of nonviolence, revealed in Jesus, can continue to be realized now. The nonviolent Jesus invites us to take up this challenge anew.

Conclusion

THE God of nonviolence invites us to live a life of steadfast, active nonviolence. God's nonviolent alternative gives us a way out of the world's addiction to violence, injustice, and death. It is a way to become sober people of nonviolence; a way to transform the world's systemic violence into justice and peace. God is disarming our hearts and our world. We are invited to cooperate with the nonviolence and disarming love of God and thus disarm the world.

The vow of nonviolence is a way to cooperate with God. It pledges that we will give our lives to God's nonviolent struggle for justice and peace. It promises that we will enter into God's transformation of our hearts and our world. It vows that we will try to be faithful to the peacemaking Jesus, to resist systemic injustice through active nonviolence, and thus to join him in his campaign of revolutionary nonviolence.

We commit ourselves to live in nonviolence all our days. We will follow the lead of God's Spirit of nonviolence. As we cooperate with God's grace, we can let go of all control, be at peace, resist systemic violence, and trust that God is making us instruments of peace.

After professing a vow of nonviolence, I was led into the world of the poor and the oppressed. In confronting the realities of violence and fear, I have tried to remember that we are all brothers and sisters and that I am invited to love all those I encounter, including those who point machine guns at me, question my solidarity with the poor, and arrest me for disturbing the peace.

I have been arrested many times for nonviolent civil disobedience at places of systemic violence. At such times I discovered that my heart was being further disarmed, that I was receiving the risen Jesus' gift of peace. In places of powerlessness and violence, I have felt an inner peace that inspires me to forgive and love, even the declared enemies of my country.

The vow of nonviolence has been a channel of grace to open my heart to the nonviolent love of God. The vow has empowered me to resist the systems of death and publicly proclaim God's reign of nonviolence. I have a long way to go on this journey. I am a sinner who still gives into the spirit of violence. But through the vow of nonviolence, God calls me deeper into Jesus' Spirit and life of active nonviolence. This invitation is compelling and exciting. I am more and more eager to pursue Jesus' way of nonviolence, to participate in God's nonviolent transformation of the world.

The choice today as Martin Luther King said, is between nonviolence or nonexistence. We can give in to the world's addiction to violence, give up the possibility of a new world of justice and peace, and go down the descending spiral of violence and despair. Or we can follow Jesus Christ, the way of nonviolence.

When we make a daily choice for Christ's nonviolence, we choose to take greater risks for justice and peace, to pursue nonviolence with greater passion, and to trust in the God of peace. To follow Jesus is to practice Jesus' way of active nonviolence. Jesus invites us to a deeper practice of nonviolence in our hearts, with our families and friends, in our communities, and in the world.

The vow of nonviolence pledges that we will join Jesus' campaign of nonviolence with wholehearted dedication. It promises that we will pursue the nonviolent reign of God just as Mohandas Gandhi, Dorothy Day, Martin Luther King, Jr., Thomas Merton, Franz Jagerstatter, Oscar Romero, Ignacio Ellacuria, Ita Ford, Maura Clarke, Dorothy Kazel, Jean Donovan, and thousands of others have done. The vow empowers us with the conviction that, when rooted in Jesus' spirit of nonviolence, even seemingly small or ineffective actions will contribute to God's nonviolent transformation of the world.

After a life of solitude and contemplation, Thomas Merton concluded that the duty of the Christian today is to work "for the total abolition of war." He wrote in *The Catholic Worker* in 1964 that the church must

> lead the way on the road to nonviolent settlement of difficulties and toward the gradual abolition of war as the way of settling international or civil disputes. Christians must become active in every possible way. . . . Prayer and sacrifice must be used as the most effective spiritual weapons in the war against war, and like all weapons, they must be used with deliberate aim: not just with a vague aspiration for peace and security, but against violence and war. This implies that we are also willing to sacrifice and restrain our own instinct for violence and aggressiveness in our relations with other people. . . . This is the great Christian task of our time.

Hours before Merton died in Bangkok, he told another participant at the interfaith conference he was attending,

"What we are asked to do at present is not so much to speak of Christ as to let him live in us so that people may find him by feeling how he lives in us."[1]

The vow of nonviolence is one way to pursue the work of peacemaking, ending war, and resisting injustice. It is one way of living so rooted in the nonviolence of Christ that we can become transparent, so people can see the nonviolent Christ living through us. The nonviolence of the vowed life permeates every facet of our lives and take us ever further into God's reign of nonviolence.

By vowing nonviolence, we accept the way, the truth, and the life of nonviolence which is Jesus himself. We recognize that we are sons and daughters of God, a people disarmed by God who want to be faithful and continue to choose God's nonviolence and loving disarmament. If many of us profess and live out a vow of nonviolence, we may help bring the Christian community back to the early life of active nonviolence.

When active nonviolence becomes explicitly connected with Christian living, when it is the norm of Christian life, when the church becomes a community of active nonviolence and steadfast resistance to systemic injustice— then vows of nonviolence will no longer be necessary. Until that day they may help us get back on the gospel's narrow path of nonviolence.

The vow of nonviolence is an invitation to enter God's reign of nonviolence. It invites us to allow God to disarm our hearts and to participate in God's disarmament of the world, to be transformed by God and thus to help transform humanity. Whether we profess the vow or not, may we all grow in the Spirit of God's nonviolence and learn to live together in God's reign of justice and peace.

Prayer for a Disarmed Heart

God of nonviolence,
thank you for your love and your gift of peace.
Give me the grace and the courage
    to live a life of nonviolence
so that I may be faithful to Jesus our peacemaker.
Send me your Spirit of nonviolence
    that I may love everyone
as my sister and my brother and not fear or hurt anyone.
Help me to be an instrument of your peace;
to struggle for justice and work to end war;
to respond with love and not to retaliate with violence;
to accept suffering in the struggle for justice
and never to inflict suffering or death on others;
to live more simply and to accompany the poor;
to resist systemic violence and death;
to choose life for all your children.
Guide me along the way of nonviolence.
Help me to speak the truth of peace,
    to practice compassion,
to act justly and to walk with you
in a contemplative spirit of nonviolent love.
Disarm my heart
and I shall be your instrument
to disarm other hearts.
Lead me, God of nonviolence,
    with the whole human family
into your nonviolent reign of justice and peace
where there is no fear, no war, no injustice,
    and no violence.
I ask this in the name of Jesus, the Way of nonviolence.
Amen.

Questions for Prayerful Reflection

1. What are my definitions of violence and nonviolence? What have been my most challenging, exciting, energizing experiences of nonviolence in my life? How have I practiced gospel nonviolence with my family and friends, in my work and community, in my city and nation?

2. How is nonviolence a struggle for me? What areas of violence in my life need to be transformed? How do I respond to violence, injustice, and war? How do I support the systems of violence which kill people and oppress most of humanity? Who do I need to be reconciled with, in my family, friendships, community, city, nation, and in the world? How has my faith, my nonviolence, and my life become routine? What I can do to break the cycle of violence and participate more in God's reign of nonviolence?

3. What has been my experience of God? Where do I encounter the peacemaking God in my day-to-day life? Do I experience God as violent, wrathful, warmaking, and mean? Or do I experience God as nonviolent, unconditionally loving, peaceful, and peacemaking? What are images of God for me?

4. What does the nonviolence of Jesus mean for me? Given today's worldwide addiction to violence, what does it mean to be a follower of Jesus who made peace, promoted justice for the poor, and resisted systemic violence with the transforming love of nonviolence?

5. How have I allowed God to disarm my heart and how am I resisting God's disarming action in my heart and in the world? Why do I arm my heart and how can I participate in God's disarming love more? How am I being called to go deeper into the active nonviolence of God?

6. What am I afraid of? Loss of reputation, loss of control, powerlessness, having my life disrupted, alienation, loneliness, poverty, jail, pain, violence, death? How willing am I to serve others without the desire for reciprocation and to accept suffering (even unto death like Jesus on the cross) without the desire for retaliation?

7. How am I already living a nonviolent life? In what areas, could I become more consistent? How am I doing in such areas as simple lifestyle, daily prayer, solidarity with the poor, public activity for justice, letting go of self-righteousness and control, spiritual direction, community, study of nonviolence and the issues of injustice, worship and Bible study, and taking new risks in nonviolence?

8. How public have I been willing to go with God's good news of nonviolence and peace? How can I further stand up publicly in the Spirit of love and proclaim the truth of nonviolence, justice, and peace? Could I risk arrest in a prayerful act of nonviolent civil disobedience to systemic violence at a place of governmental or nuclear violence? How could I further practice the illegal Christian peacemaking which Jesus modeled? What does it mean for me to take up the cross of nonviolent resistance to injustice and practice nonviolence?

9. What further concrete steps can I take along God's way of active nonviolence? Where might God be calling me to take new risks, to enter deeper waters, to walk out farther on the water of nonviolence?

10. Am I committed to nonviolence for the long haul? How could I pursue a deeper, long-haul commitment, spirituality, and life of Gospel nonviolence? What attracts me to the vow of nonviolence? What challenges me?

Scripture Passages for Meditation and Reflection on Nonviolence

Deuteronomy 30:15-20
2 Maccabees 7:1-42
Psalms 85, 86, 91
Song of Solomon 2:10b-14
Wisdom 7:7-11
Sirach (Ecclesiasticus)
    2:1–11
Isaiah 2:1-5; 9:1-6; 11:1-9;
    42:1-9; 43:1-7, 15-21;
    49:1-6, 8-16; 52:7;
    53:1-12; 58:1-12;
    61:1-4; 65:17-25
Jeremiah 1:4-10
Lamentations 3:17-33,
    40–41
Ezekiel 37:1-14
Daniel 3:1-97; 6:2-28
Joel 2:12-17
Amos 5:14-15
Jonah 1:1-4:11
Micah 4:1-8; 6:8
Matthew 5:1-48; 6:1-34;
    7:1-29; 10:16-39;
    11:28-29; 12:9-14;
    13:31-33; 16:24-26;
    19:16-30; 22:34-40;
    25:31-46; 26:36-75;
    27:1-56
Mark 1:12-15; 9:33-41;
    10:17-52; 11:15-19;
    12:13-17; 14:32-72;
    15:1-16:8
Luke 1:46-55, 67-79;
    4:16–30; 6:20-49;

9:18–36, 51-62; 12:3-9,
    13-34; 13:22-35;
    15:11–32; 16:19-31;
    18:18-43; 19:41-48;
    22:39-71; 23:1-56;
    24:1-53
John 8:1-11; 12:23-33;
    13:1–17; 15:1-17;
    18:1–40; 19:1-37;
    20:11-29; 21:1-19
Acts of the Apostles 3:1-26;
    4:1-35; 5:17-42;
    7:54–60; 16:16-40
Romans 5:1-21; 8:18-39;
    12:1-21; 13:8-10
1 Corinthians 1:18-31;
    12:1–31; 13:1-13;
    15:54-58
2 Corinthians 4:1-18;
    5:17–21; 6:1-10
Galatians 6:1-10
Ephesians 1:3-14; 2:13-22;
    4:1-6, 25-32; 5:1-20;
    6:10-18
Philippians 2:1-18; 4:4-9
Colossians 3:5-17
Hebrews 12:1-15
James 1:2-18,22; 2:1-26;
    3:17-18; 4:1-17; 5:1-12
1 Peter 1:13-16, 22-25;
    2:1–10; 3:8-18; 4:7-19
2 John 3:1-3; 4:7-21
Revelation 21:1-8

Notes

Chapter 1

1. Thomas McDonnell, ed., *A Thomas Merton Reader* (New York: Image Books, 1974), 276.

2. Daniel Berrigan, *Steadfastness of the Saints* (Maryknoll, N.Y.: Orbis, 1985), 3.

3. John Dear, ed., *It's a Sin to Build a Nuclear Weapon: The Collected Works on War and Christian Peacemaking of Richard McSorley* (Baltimore, Md.: Fortkamp Pub. Co., 1991), 97.

4. Charles McCarthy, *Christian Nonviolence: Option or Obligation?* (Unpublished, transcript of video series, available from AGAPE, 918 North Main Street, Brockton, MA 02401), 6-1.

5. Tom Abate. "Physicist Issues Call to Arms as Lab Turns 40," *San Francisco Examiner*, September 2, 1992, A3.

6. McCarthy, ibid., 8-5.

7. Coretta Scott King, ed., *The Words of Martin Luther King, Jr.* (New York: Newmarket Press, 1983), 73.

8. Thomas Gumbleton, "Peacemaking as a Way of Life," in John Coleman, ed., *One Hundred Years of Catholic Social Thought* (Maryknoll, N.Y.: Orbis, 1991), 309-310.

9. Ibid., 311-312.

10. Ibid., 313-315.

Chapter 2

1. Stephen B. Oates, *Let the Trumpet Sound: The Life of Martin Luther King, Jr.* (New York: New American Lib., 1982), 89-90.

2. Ibid.

3. Elizabeth McAlister, "Foreword," in John Dear, *Our God Is Nonviolent* (New York: Pilgrim Press, 1990), xiv.

4. McCarthy, 10-14.

5. Martin Luther King, Jr., *Stride Toward Freedom* (New York: Harper & Row, 1958), 84.

6. King, *Stride Toward Freedom*, 87-88.

7. Gerard Vanderhaar, *Nonviolence: Theory and Practice* (Erie, Pa.: Pax Christi, USA, 1980), 6.

8. *Peacemaking Day by Day* (Erie, Pa.: Pax Christi USA, 1985), 5.

9. Thomas Merton, *Gandhi on Nonviolence* (New York: New Directions, 1964), 45.

10. Ibid., 28.

11. *The Words of Martin Luther King, Jr.*, 72.

Chapter 3

1. *The Code of Canon Law* (Grand Rapids: Eerdmans,1983), 210.

Chapter 4

1. *The Catholic Agitator*, July 1989, 7.

2. McCarthy, 1-11.

3. Joseph Fahey, *Peace, War and the Christian Conscience* (Christopher Publications, 1982), 10.

4. Gerard Vanderhaar, *Christians and Nonviolence in the Nuclear Age* (Mystic, Conn.: Twenty-Third Pub., 1983), 16-18.

5. Ibid., 22; Jim Wallis, ed., *Waging Peace* (San Francisco: Harper & Row, 1981), 2.

6. For further study on the U.S. bombings of Hiroshima and Nagasaki, and a U.S. intelligence report in the National Archives that contradicts the popular notion that the United States had to drop nuclear weapons on Japan, see Gar Alperovitz, *Atomic Diplomacy: Hiroshima and Potsdam* (New York: Simon and Schuster, 1965). For a short synopsis of his research, see "Did We Have to Drop the Bomb?" by Gar Alperovitz in the editorial section of the *New York Times*, August 3, 1989.

For further reading, see Arthur J. Laffin and Anne Montgomery, *Swords into Plowshares* (San Francisco: Harper & Row, 1987); Robert Aldridge, *First Strike* (Boston: South End, 1983); Robert Aldridge, *Nuclear Empire* (Vancouver: New Star Books, 1989); Michio Kaku and

Daniel Axelrod, *To Win a Nuclear War* (Boston: South End Press, 1987); and Jim Wallis, ed., *Waging Peace* (San Francisco: Harper & Row, 1982).

7. Vanderhaar, *Christians and Nonviolence*, 25.

8. "To Be or Not To Be" (Christopher Publications, 1981); *Newsweek*, December 5, 1983, 56.

9. Vanderhaar, *Christians and Nonviolence*, 28.

10. See W. Brandt, *North-South*, MIT Press, 1980; United Nations Press Release; Disarmament Fact Sheet, Public Relations, UN Document A/35/392; East African Fact Sheet: American Friends Service Committee; Presidential Commission Report on World Hunger, 1981. For the latest statistics on world violence and injustice, see Ruth Leger Sivard, *World Military and Social Expenditures 1992* (Washington, D.C.: World Priorities, 1992).

11. For further reading, see James Douglass, *The Nonviolent Coming of God* (Maryknoll, N.Y.: Orbis Books, 1991), 10-12.

12. For further reading, see James Douglass, *Lightning East to West* (New York: Crossroad, 1984), 73-97.

13. For further information contact Bread for the World, 802 Rhode Island Ave. N.E., Washington, D.C. 20018 (202 269-0200).

14. See Jack Nelson-Pallmeyer, *War Against the Poor: Low-Intensity Conflict and Christian Faith* (Maryknoll, N.Y.: Orbis Books, 1989); also, John Dear, *Jean Donovan and the Call to Discipleship* and *Oscar Romero and the Nonviolent Struggle for Justice*, both available from Pax Christi USA, 348 East Tenth St., Erie, PA 16508.

15. See Tom Fox, *Iraq* (Kansas City, MO: Sheed and Ward, 1991); Jack Nelson-Pallmeyer, *Brave New World Order* (Maryknoll, New York: Orbis Books, 1992).

16. Edward Rice, *The Man in the Sycamore Tree* (New York: Doubleday, 1970), 89.

17. Martin Luther King, Jr., *Why We Can't Wait* (New York: Mentor Books, 1963), 63-64.

18. John Howard Yoder, "Living the Disarmed Life," in Jim Wallis, ed., *Waging Peace*, 132.

Chapter 5

1. Joseph Martos, *Doors to the Sacred* (New York: Image Books, 1982), 11-12.

2. Ibid.

3. See *The Rites of the Catholic Church*. Vol. I (New York: Pueblo Pub., 1990), 223-226.

4. James Douglass, *Lightning East to West* (New York: Crossroad, 1983), 7; and Merton, *Gandhi on Nonviolence*, 6.

5. Daniel Berrigan, *To Dwell In Peace: An Autobiography* (San Francisco: Harper & Row, 1987), 163-164.

6. John Dear, *Seeds of Nonviolence* (Baltimore, Md.: Fortkamp Pub. Co., 1992), 197.

Chapter 6

1. Merton, *Gandhi on Nonviolence*, 29.

2. "Nonviolent Direct Action," published by the International Fellowship of Reconciliation, December 1983.

3. Merton, *Gandhi on Nonviolence*, 4, 6, 9-10, 18-20, 28-29, 33.

4. Mohandas Gandhi, *All Men Are Brothers* (New York: Continuum, 1980), 89.

5. John Kavanaugh, *Following Christ in a Consumer Society* (Maryknoll: Orbis Books, 1981), 121-122.

6. Mohandas Gandhi, *An Autobiography* (Boston: Beacon Press, 1957), 1-6.

7. See George Aschenbrenner, "Comparison and Competition: Stifling Spiritual Intimacy," *Review for Religious,* vol. 38, no. 6, 1979, 924-931.

8. Jim Wallis, *Revive Us Again: A Sojourner's Story* (Nashville: Abingdon Press, 1983), 155-156.

9. Gandhi, *An Autobiography.*

Chapter 7

1. Roland Bainton, *Christian Attitudes Toward War and Peace* (New York: Abingdon Press, 1960), 66-84.

2. C. John Cadoux, *The Early Christian Attitude to War* (New York: Seabury, 1982), 245.

3. Bainton, ibid.; Mary Lou Kownacki, "A Vow of Nonviolence," *The Christian Witness*, (Erie, Pa.: Winter 1985).

Chapter 8

1. Martin Luther King, Jr. "Pilgrimage to Nonviolence," *A Testament of Hope*, James Washington ed., (San Francisco: Harper & Row, 1986), 38.

2. *The Words of Martin Luther King, Jr.*, 71.

3. Merton, *Gandhi on Nonviolence*, 44.

4. Ibid., 25.

5. Ibid.

6. Ibid., 32.

7. Ibid., 33.

8. Ibid., 32.

9. Richard Attenborough, ed., *The Words of Gandhi* (New York: Newmarket Press, 1982), 10.

10. Eknath Easwaran, *Gandhi the Man* (Berkeley: Nilgiri Press, 1978), 16.

11. Merton, *Gandhi on Nonviolence*, 24.

12. Ibid., 39.

13. Ibid., 44.

14. *The Words of Gandhi*, 10.

15. James Douglass, *The Non-Violent Cross* (New York: Macmillan, 1968), 34.

16. Gandhi, *An Autobiography*, 180-181.

17. Calvin Kytle, *Gandhi, Soldier of Nonviolence* (Washington, D.C.: Seven Locks Press, 1982), 90-91; Louis Fischer, *The Life of Mahatma Gandhi* (New York: Harper & Row, 1950), 75-76.

18. Fischer, 177.

19. Mohandas Gandhi, *Nonviolent Resistance* (New York: Schocken Books, 1951), iii.

20. Ibid., 37-38.

21. Merton, *Gandhi on Nonviolence*, 26.

22. Ibid., 52.

23. Ibid., 24.

24. Ibid., 29.

25. Easwaran, *Gandhi the Man*, 129.

26. Ibid., 155.

27. Gandhi, *All Men Are Brothers*, 87.

28. *The Words of Gandhi*, 44.

29. Easwaran, *Gandhi the Man*, 56.

30. Merton, *Gandhi on Nonviolence*, 68.

31. Ibid., 32.

32. Gandhi, *All Men Are Brothers*, 49.

33. Ibid., 50.

34. Douglass, *Lightning East to West*, 17-40.

35. Gandhi, *All Men Are Brothers*, 54.

36. Vincent Sheean, *Lead, Kindly Light* (New York: Random House, 1949), 186.

37. Louis Fischer, *Gandhi: His Life and Message for the World* (New York: Mentor Books, 1954), 18.

38. Merton, *Gandhi on Nonviolence*. Ibid., 6.

39. Thomaa Merton, *The Nonviolent Alternative* (New York: Farrar, Straus, Giroux, 1971, 1980), 178-184; Merton, *Gandhi on Nonviolence*, 20.

40. Merton, *The Nonviolent Alternative*, 178-184.

41. Merton, *Gandhi on Nonviolence*, 26, 34, 40.

Chapter 9

1. Ched Myers, *Binding the Strong Man: A Political Reading of Mark's Story of Jesus* (Maryknoll: Orbis Books,1988), 57; see also Jim Douglass, *The Nonviolent Coming of God*, 70-72.

2. Douglass, Ibid., 72.

3. Walter Wink, *Violence and Nonviolence in South Africa: Jesus' Third Way* (Philadelphia: New Society Pub., 1987), 16.

4. Ibid., 17.

5. Ibid., 18-19.

6. Ibid., 20-22.

7. For a more thorough presentation of Jesus' nonviolent resistance, study Ched Myers' book, *Binding the Strong Man*. (See also my chapter on the life and nonviolent resistance of Jesus, in my book, *Our God Is Nonviolent*, 38-45.)

8. Myers, 299-302; Dear, *Our God Is Nonviolent*, 41-43; also Bill Kellerman, "The Cleansing of the Temple," in Jim Wallis, ed, *The Rise of Christian Conscience* (San Francisco: Harper & Row, 1987), 256-261.

Conclusion

1. James Forest, *Thomas Merton* (New York: Paulist Press, 1980), 73-79, 99.

Suggested Readings

Aldridge, Robert. *First Strike! The Pentagon's Plan for Nuclear War.* Boston: South End Press, 1983.

_____. *Nuclear Empire.* Vancouver: New Star Books, 1989.

An Interrupted Life: The Diaries of Etty Hillesum. New York: Washington Square Press, 1981.

Bainton, Roland. *Christian Attitudes Toward War and Peace.* New York: Abingdon, 1960.

Berrigan, Daniel. *Ten Commandments for the Long Haul.* Nashville: Abingdon, 1981.

_____. *The Nightmare of God.* Baltimore, Md.: Fortkamp Pub., 1983, 1991.

_____. *To Dwell in Peace: An Autobiography.* San Francisco: Harper & Row, 1987.

_____. *Uncommon Prayer.* New York: Winston/Seabury, 1978.

_____. *Whereon to Stand: The Acts of the Apostles and Ourselves.* Baltimore, Md.: Fortkamp Pub., 1991.

Berrigan, Philip. *Widen the Prison Gates.* New York: Simon and Schuster, 1973.

Berrigan, Philip and Elizabeth McAlister. *The Time's Discipline: The Beatitudes and Nuclear Resistance.* Baltimore: Fortkamp Pub., 1989.

Bondurant, Joan. *Conquest of Violence: The Gandhian Philosophy of Conflict.* Berkeley: Univ. of Cal. Press, 1969.

Bonhoeffer, Dietrich. *The Cost of Discipleship.* New York: Macmillan/Collier, 1937, 1977.

Brockman, James. *Romero: A Life.* Maryknoll: Orbis, 1990.

Brown, Robert McAfee. *Spirituality and Liberation.* Philadelphia: The Westminster Press, 1986.

_____. *Unexpected News.* Philadelphia: The Westminster Press, 1984.

Cadoux, C. John. *The Early Christian Attitude to War.* New York: Seabury, 1982.

Camara, Helder. *The Spiral of Violence.* New York: Sheed and Ward, 1971.

Day, Dorothy. *The Long Loneliness.* New York: Harper & Row, 1981.

_____. *Loaves and Fishes.* San Francisco: Harper & Row, 1983.

Dear, John. *Jean Donovan: The Call to Discipleship.* (Available from Pax Christi, 348 East Tenth St., Erie, PA 16503.) 1986.

_____. *Oscar Romero and the Nonviolent Struggle for Justice* Erie, Pa.: Pax Christi USA, 1990.

_____. *Our God Is Nonviolent.* New York: Pilgrim Press, 1990.

_____. *Seeds of Nonviolence.* Baltimore, Md.: Fortkamp Pub., 1992. (To order, call 1 800-43-PEACE.)

Dear, John with Joe Hines, eds. *Christ Is with the Poor: Stories and Sayings of Horace McKenna, SJ.* (Available from McKenna Center, 19 Eye Street NW, Washington, DC 20001.)

Douglass, James. *Lightning East to West.* New York: Crossroad, 1983.

_____. *Resistance and Contemplation.* New York: Doubleday, 1971.

_____. *The Nonviolent Coming of God.* Maryknoll: Orbis, 1991.

_____. *The Nonviolent Cross.* New York: Macmillan, 1968.

Easwaran, Eknath. *Gandhi the Man.* Berkeley: Nilgiri Press, 1978.

Ellsberg, Robert, ed. *Dorothy Day: Selected Writings.* Maryknoll: Orbis Books, 1992.

_____. *Gandhi on Christianity*. Maryknoll: Orbis, 1991.

Erikson, Erik. *Gandhi's Truth*. New York: Norton, 1969.

Finney, Torin. *Unsung Hero of the Great War: The Life and Witness of Ben Salmon*. Mahwah, N.J.: Paulist Press, 1989.

Fischer, Louis. *The Life of Mahatma Gandhi*. New York: Harper & Row, 1950, 1982.

Forest, Jim. *Living With Wisdom: A Life of Thomas Merton*. Maryknoll: Orbis Books, 1991.

_____. *Love Is the Measure: A Biography of Dorothy Day*. Mahwah, N.J.: Paulist Press, 1986.

Fuller, R. and I., eds. *Essays on the Love Commandment*. Philadelphia: Fortress, 1978.

Gandhi, Mohandas. *All Men Are Brothers*. New York: Continuum, 1982.

_____. *An Autobiography or The Story of My Experiments in Truth*. Beacon, 1957.

Gallagher, Michael. *Laws of Heaven*. New York: Ticknor and Fields, 1992.

Grannis, Christopher, Arthur Laffin, and Elin Schade. *The Risk of the Cross*. New York: Seabury, 1981.

Gregg, Richard. *The Power of Nonviolence*. New York: Schocken, 1966.

Gutiérrez, Gustavo. *A Theology of Liberation*. Maryknoll: Orbis Books, 1973.

_____. *The Power of the Poor in History*. Maryknoll: Orbis Books, 1983.

_____. *We Drink from Our Own Wells*. Maryknoll: Orbis Books, 1983.

Hanh, Thich Nhat. *Being Peace*. Berkeley: Parallex Press, 1987.

Häring, Bernard. *Dare to Be Christian*. Liguori, Miss.: Liguori, 1983.

Hauerwas, Stanley. *The Peaceable Kingdom: A Primer in Christian Ethics*. South Bend, Ind.: Univ. of Notre Dame Press, 1983.

Hellwig, Monika. *Jesus: The Compassion of God*. Wilmington: Michael Glazier, 1984.

_____. *The Eucharist and the Hunger of the World*. New York: Paulist Press, 1976.

Hersey, John. *Hiroshima*. New York: Alfred A. Knopf, 1946.

Hollyday, Joyce. *Turning Toward Home*. San Francisco: Harper & Row, 1989.

Jesudasan, Ignatius. *A Gandhian Theology of Liberation*. Maryknoll: Orbis Books, 1984.

Kaku, Michio and Daniel Axelrod. *To Win a Nuclear War: The Pentagon's Secret War Plans*. Boston: South End Press, 1987.

Kavanaugh, John Francis. *Following Christ in a Consumer Society: The Spirituality of Cultural Resistance*. Maryknoll: Orbis Books, 1991.

King, Martin Luther Jr., *Strength to Love*. Philadelphia: Fortress, 1963, 1981.

_____. *Stride Toward Freedom*. New York: Harper & Row, 1958.

_____. *Where Do We Go from Here?* New York: Harper & Row, 1967.

_____. *Why We Can't Wait*. New York: Mentor, 1963.

Kyle, Calvin. *Gandhi, Soldier of Nonviolence*. Washington, D.C.: Seven Locks, 1982.

Laffin, Arthur J., and Anne Montgomery. *Swords into Plowshares* San Francisco: Harper & Row, 1987.

Macgregor, G. H. C. *The New Testament Basis of Pacifism*. New York: Fellowship, 1941, 1971.

Matura, Thadee. *Gospel Radicalism*. Maryknoll: Orbis, 1984.

McGinnis, James and Kathleen. *Parenting for Peace and Justice*. Maryknoll: Orbis Books, 1981.

McKenzie, John. *The Power and the Wisdom*. New York: Bruce, 1965.

McNeal, Patricia. *Harder than War*. New Brunswick, N.J.: Rutgers Univ. Press, 1992.

McSorley, Richard. *New Testament Basis of Peacemaking*. Scottdale, Pa.: Herald Press, 1985.

_____. *It's a Sin to Build a Nuclear Weapon*. (John Dear, Ed.) Baltimore, Md.: Fortkamp Pub., 1990.

Merton, Thomas. *Conjectures of a Guilty Bystander*. New York: Doubleday, 1966.

_____. ed. *Gandhi on Nonviolence*. New York: New Directions, 1961.

_____. *New Seeds of Contemplation*. New York: New Directions, 1961.

_____. *The Hidden Ground of Love: Letters*. William Shannon, ed. New York: Farrar, Straus and Giroux, 1985.

_____. *The Nonviolent Alternative*. New York: Farrar, Straus, and Giroux, 1971, 1980.

_____. *The Road to Joy: Letters*. New York: Farrar, Straus, and Giroux, 1989.

_____. *The School of Charity: Letters*. New York: Farrar, Straus, and Giroux, 1990.

Miller, William Robert. *Nonviolence*. New York: Schocken, 1964.

Musto, Ronald. *The Catholic Peace Tradition*. Maryknoll: Orbis Books, 1986.

Myers, Ched. *Binding the Strong Man: A Political Reading of Mark's Story of Jesus*. Maryknoll: Orbis Books, 1988.

Nelson-Pallmeyer, Jack. *Brave New World Order*. Maryknoll: Orbis Books, 1992.

_____. *War Against the Poor: Low-Intensity Conflict and Christian Faith*. Maryknoll: Orbis Books, 1989.

Nouwen, Henri. *In the Name of Jesus*. New York: Crossroad, 1988.

Oates, Stephen. *Let the Trumpet Sound: The Life of Martin Luther King, Jr*. New York: Plume, 1982.

Quigley, Margaret and Michael Garvey. *The Dorothy Day Book*. Springfield, Ill.: Templegate Publ., 1982.

Rice, Edward. *The Man in the Sycamore Tree*. New York: Doubleday, 1970.

Romero, Oscar. *The Violence of Love*. San Francisco: Harper & Row, 1988.

Schell, Jonathan. *The Fate of the Earth*. New York: Knopf, 1981.

Schussler Fiorenza, Elisabeth. *In Memory of Her: A Feminist Theological Reconstruction of Christian Origins*. New York: Crossroad, 1985.

Shannon, William. *Seeking the Face of God*. New York: Crossroad, 1988.

_____. *Silence on Fire*. New York: Crossroad, 1991.

Sharp, Gene. *Gandhi as Political Strategist*. Boston: Porter Sargent, 1979.

_____. *The Politics of Nonviolent Action* (3 vols.) Boston: Porter Sargent, 1973.

Sider, Ron, *Christ and Violence*. Scottdale, Pa.; Herald Press, 1979.

Sider, Ron, and Richard Taylor. *Nuclear Holocaust and Christian Hope*. Downers Grove, Ill.: InterVarsity, 1982.

Sobrino, Jon and Ignacio Ellacuria. *Companions of Jesus*. Maryknoll: Orbis Books, 1990.

Solle, Dorothee. *Of War and Love*. Maryknoll: Orbis Books, 1981.

Stringfellow, William. *An Ethic for Christians and Other Aliens In a Strange Land*. Waco, Tex.: Word, 1973.

_____. *The Politics of Spirituality*. Philadelphia: Westminster Press, 1984.

Thoreau, Henry David. *Walden and On the Duty of Civil Disobedience*. New York: New American Library, 1960.

Tolstoy's Writings on Nonviolence and Civil Disobedience. New York: Bergman, 1967.

Trocmé, André. *Jesus and the Nonviolent Revolution*. Scottdale, Pa.: Herald Press, 1973.

True, Michael, ed. *Daniel Berrigan: Poetry, Drama, Prose*. Maryknoll: Orbis Books, 1988.

Vanderhaar, Gerard. *Christians and Nonviolence in the Nuclear Age*. Mystic, Conn.: Twenty-Third Pub., 1982.

_____. *Active Nonviolence*. Mystic, Conn.: Twenty-Third Pub., 1990.

Vanier, Jean. *Community and Growth*. New York: Paulist Press, 1979.

Wallis, Jim. *Agenda for Biblical People*. San Francisco: Harper & Row, 1984.

_____. *Revive Us Again: A Sojourner's Story*. Nashville: Abingdon, 1983.

_____. *Peacemakers*. San Francisco: Harper & Row, 1983.

_____. *The Rise of Christian Conscience*. San Francisco: Harper & Row, 1987.

_____. ed. *Waging Peace*. San Francisco: Harper & Row, 1982.

Wallis, Jim, and Joyce Hollyday. *Cloud of Witnesses*. Maryknoll: Orbis Books, 1991.

Washington, James M., *A Testament of Hope: The Essential Writings of Martin Luther King, Jr*. San Francisco: Harper & Row, 1986.

Wilcox, Fred. *Uncommon Martyrs: The Plowshares Movement*. New York: Addison-Wesley Pub. Co., 1991.

Wink, Walter. *Violence and Nonviolence in South Africa: Jesus' Third Way*. Philadelphia: New Society Pub., 1987.

_____. *Engaging the Powers*. Philadelphia: Fortress Press, 1992.

_____. *Naming the Powers*. Philadelphia: Fortress Press, 1984.

_____. *Unmasking the Powers*. Philadelphia: Fortress Press, 1987.

Yoder, John Howard, *Nevertheless*. Scottdale, Pa.: Herald Press, 1983.

_____. *The Politics of Jesus*. Grand Rapids, Mich: Eerdmans Pub., 1972.

_____. *What Would You Do?* Scottdale, Pa.: Herald Press, 1983.

_____. *When War Is Unjust*. Augsburg Press, 1983.

Zahn, Gordon. *In Solitary Witness: The Life and Death of Franz Jagerstatter*. Collegeville, Minn.: The Liturgical Press, 1964.

The Author

JOHN Dear is a Jesuit priest, peace activist, and organizer who works to promote Christian nonviolence. He holds degrees from the Jesuit School of Theology at the Graduate Theological Union in Berkeley, California.

His books include *Seeds of Nonviolence* (Fortkamp, 1992), *Our God Is Nonviolent: Witnesses in the Struggle for Peace and Justice* (Pilgrim Press, 1990), *Jean Donovan: The Call to Discipleship* (Pax Christi, 1986), and *Oscar Romero and the Nonviolent Struggle for Justice* (Pax Christ USA, 1991). He has written extensively on peace and justice issues for such publications as *Sojourners, America, The National Catholic Reporter, Fellowship, The Catholic Worker, The Other Side,* and *The New Oxford Review.*

Dear currently works with the homeless at the Horace McKenna Center and St. Aloysius' Church in Washington, D.C. He has also served suffering people in a church-run refugee camp in El Salvador, has organized and demonstrated nonviolently for an end to the arms race and to war at numerous U.S. military bases, and has worked to abolish the death penalty. Extensive travels to witness for peace have taken him across the U.S. as well as to such areas as Central America, the Middle East, Haiti, and the Philippines.

Dear gives lectures and retreats on Christian non-violence and peacemaking across the U.S. He serves on the national councils of Pax Christi USA and the Fellowship of Reconciliation. He is a member of the board of directors of the Nevada Desert Experience, a Christian witness to stop the testing of nuclear weapons. He is chair of the annual Pax Christi USA Book Award.